The Question

The Question

*A Survey of the Questions Asked
by the World's Most Influential Leader*

Jim Way

WIPF & STOCK · Eugene, Oregon

THE QUESTION
A Survey of the Questions Asked by the World's Most Influential Leader

Copyright © 2009 Jim Way. All rights reserved. Except for brief quotations in critical publications or reviews, no part of this book may be reproduced in any manner without prior written permission from the publisher. Write: Permissions, Wipf and Stock Publishers, 199 W. 8th Ave., Suite 3, Eugene, OR 97401.

Wipf & Stock
A Division of Wipf and Stock Publishers
199 W. 8th Ave., Suite 3
Eugene, OR 97401
www.wipfandstock.com

ISBN 13: 978-1-60608-229-4

All scripture quotations, unless otherwise indicated, are taken from the New King James Version®. Copyright © 1982 by Thomas Nelson, Inc. Used by permission. All rights reserved.

Scripture quotations marked (NIV) are taken from the HOLY BIBLE, NEW INTERNATIONAL VERSION®. NIV®. Copyright © 1973, 1978, 1984 by International Bible Society. Used by permission of Zondervan. All rights reserved. (Italics used in quotations from Scripture have been inserted by the author).

Manufactured in the U.S.A.

Contents

Foreword vii
Preface ix
Introduction xi

1 Spiritual Values 1

2 Spiritual Life 12

3 Spiritual Relationships 23

4 Spiritual Alignment 32

5 Spiritual Commitment 44

6 Spiritual Provisions 54

7 Spiritual Revelations 64

8 Spiritual Warnings 76

   Conclusion 85

   Appendix 87
   —Questions in Chronological Order

Foreword

THIS BOOK is unique. It was written by a follower of Christ to enlighten other followers or would-be followers. There are more than 230 questions recorded in Scripture that Jesus asked the people. After examining these questions, the author sets forth two main purposes for his book.

First, Jesus confronted people with questions that exposed the root cause of their problems. His question caused them to answer for themselves the issues they faced.

The second purpose for the book is to show the relevance of Jesus's questions for our day. With his decades of experience in the business world and as a corporate church leader, Jim desires the church, parent, boss, CEO, teacher, and coach to deal with current problems that face our culture.

This book sees great relevance in the questions posed by Jesus for our present-day turmoil, either directly or indirectly. Jim attempts to catch the significance of this extraordinary teaching device of Jesus.

Two audiences will be informed and encouraged by this book. First, those who have been disenchanted with the emphasis today on crowds and platform-style performances accompanied by the lack of accountability and spiritual effectiveness of the modern-day bureaucracy of church culture will be encouraged by the book. The reader who loves Jesus often does not see Jesus in his church. Thus, many of Jesus's questions can be applied to church members today.

Second, Jesus simultaneously inspired his followers and challenged religious leaders. The latter will find this book convicting. But the former will find this book inspiring. They will identify their own problems with practices two thousand years ago. I recommend that every church member read this book and carefully apply its lessons to his or her own life today. It will help to reconnect so many businesspersons and young people who find themselves estranged from the church. They will find Jesus's message fresh and relevant after two millennia.

Jim Way sees Jesus's methods of questioning his listeners as probing, relevant, and setting the stage for fresh understanding of God's plan for his people today. He also provides a daily devotional guide for the spiritual life. Read with the proper attitude, this book can cause you to search your motives and re-examine your methods of doing God's work today. "For the word of God *is* living and powerful, and sharper than any two-edged sword, piercing even to the division of soul and spirit, and of joints and marrow, and is a discerner of the thoughts and intents of the heart" (Heb 4:12).

I recommend that you take time to read this book. It will provide new insights, not only into Jesus's provocative and penetrating questions but also into the condition of your own heart. It will provide a pertinent plan for altering our priorities in view of Jesus's questions. As most everyone knows, probing questions can be stimulating. And questions from the Master can be life-changing.

Dr. Norman L. Geisler
Distinguished Professor of Theology
Veritas Evangelical Seminary, Murrieta, California

Preface

Thousands of Christian books are written every year. So why write another one? I suppose, like others, I felt *led to do so*. I spent my professional life running manufacturing companies with departments of various complexities, all brought together in synergism to produce thousands of multi-level assemblies every day. Hundreds of people were focused on one objective—how many pieces per hour would go out the door.

When I entered the realm of the Church, I looked at the Church organism from this peculiar point of view. This caused me to form Renewed Life Ministries on the east coast of Florida, which grew from six churches to five hundred and thirty churches. For twenty-five years, we met for various leadership conferences, retreats, celebrations, and outreaches, whereby ten thousand people gathered numerous times at the West Palm Beach Auditorium, and hundreds of others in local churches and conference rooms. As I studied the Church and its bureaucracy, effectiveness, and productivity, I began to ask a question: did Jesus have the same problems we have today? He certainly did, and he addressed them in such a way that we know it had to come from heaven.

My deepest appreciation goes to my wife, Sherry, who has been my eyes, my ears, and my hands. Without her, this book could not have even begun. I wish to thank my son, Craig, whose literary talent far surpasses my own. I also want to thank the board of Capernaum Ministries, who continually encourage me in my work for the Lord. And to Mickey Evans, Evans Crary, Arnold Prater, and the many Church leaders who have discipled me through the years. These men invested literally hundreds of hours into a once hard-nosed production manager, raised up from the plant floor.

My hope and prayer is that *The Question* will permit Jesus to speak to your heart as he did mine concerning the modern-day dilemmas of the Church.

Introduction

Why Is The Question Unique?

Two thousand years ago, Jesus challenged the religious system of his day. It had become infiltrated with traditions and man-made practices that had nothing to do with the Word of God or the Lord's intervention for his people. Many of the people with whom Jesus came in contact had doubts and were oppressed by this religious system. Jesus challenged the people of his day by asking over 230 questions—more than any other leader in recorded history.

The uniqueness of this book is threefold: First, in two thousand years, no other book has been written that summarizes these extraordinary questions. Second, the questions that Jesus asked pressed the very heart and root of the issues that were universally significant during that period. Third, these questions, the answers to these questions, and Jesus's authentic resolutions transcend time and space to the current condition of our culture today. They cover every aspect of our lives, whether we deal with the purpose of life, our relationships to one another, or how God wants to impact our conventional society.

The Question builds a bridge between what Jesus said two thousand years ago and his empirical message to what we desperately need to hear today. Jesus has a unique way of communicating, inspiring us to reach down deep into our very being. His questions are piercing and challenging and cause introspection that could only be inspired by the Almighty. It is a unique and unusual process of communication created by the world's greatest leader.

This is not a book of answers. Thousands of books have been written about answers, instructions, and testimonies. This book is about questions—questions Jesus asked two thousand years ago and how these questions are relevant today.

BACKGROUND

I was a young industrial management consultant in my early thirties and still very impressionable. A corporate conglomerate hired me to take over a three-plant facility in north central Ohio to help restructure management and materials systems so the company would be more productive. The previous General Manager, in his last meeting with his staff, said something very profound to me as young consultant. "Decisions are not difficult," he said. "What is difficult are the questions. If you ask the right questions, you get the right answers, and if you get the right answers, you have all the right facts. Then if you have all the right facts, the decisions are obvious!"

Wow! What an astounding revelation to me. When I recommitted my life to the Lord a couple of years later, I was amazed at how many questions Jesus asked in the New Testament. Over two hundred and thirty-three questions, in fact. They were questions about all matters of life, including life itself. Many years later, I felt the inspiration to write this book.

STRUCTURE

The questions Jesus asked are categorized into eight chapters: "Spiritual Values," "Spiritual Life," "Spiritual Relationships," "Spiritual Alignment," "Spiritual Commitment," "Spiritual Provisions," "Spiritual Revelations," and "Spiritual Warnings." Each chapter is broken into three sections: "The Definition," "The Bridge," and "The Questions." In attempting to bring the reader into the perspective of what Jesus is saying in contemporary terms, the sections on "The Definition" and "The Bridge" may be somewhat lengthy, as in the "Spiritual Values" and "Spiritual Relationships" chapters.

In some chapters, these sections are very short because they require no lengthy explanation. What is important is that Jesus answers many of his own questions, and they can pierce our hearts today as they did two thousand years ago when he asked them. Often the application is quickly and uniquely apparent.

Some questions Jesus asks, he does not answer. We are left to ponder what Jesus meant and in some cases why he asked the question in the first place. *Jesus asked more questions than any other great leader in history.* In fact, when he was twelve years old, the first words Jesus ever spoke recorded in Scripture were a question that resonates through the ages: **"Why are you searching for me?"** (Luke 2:49). There must be some reason he asked all these questions. They are probing and provocative. They cause us to introspect and look deep into our motives. Jesus, with all his wisdom and practical applications, invites us into the realm of research—a laboratory full of questions.

1

Spiritual Values

The Price Tag Perspective

THE DEFINITION

Values: That quality of a thing according to which it is thought of as being more or less desirable, useful, estimable, important, etc.; worth or degree of worth. That which is desirable or worthy of esteem for its own sake; things or quality having intrinsic worth.

WEBSTER'S NEW WORLD DICTIONARY

EACH MATERIAL item we own has an appraised value. Retail stores place price tags on items according to their estimated worth. Appraisal companies obtain their values based on the assumption that each item (property, vehicles, buildings, jewelry, etc.), properly evaluated, must be independently considered on its own merit. For a vehicle, the information is gathered from new and used dealers, auto shows, trade periodicals, vehicle classifieds, magazines, newspapers, advisory boards, associations, and car clubs. Even eBay (the online market) displays an estimated value for some of the products it offers to online bidders.

Likewise, everything in life has a value or price tag. Identifying what is valuable to us helps create direction or purpose for our life, which in turn generates a sense of fulfillment and peace. Jesus created a conversational teaching style in which he asked a person or an audience a question or series of questions. He asked numerous questions in order to make people think about what was important to them. His questions probed deeply. He understood that ascertaining the true values of a person's heart required specific questions. The questions that Jesus asked could help bring into focus the priorities we have today.

God created humanity to have fellowship with him and one another. The value we place on others will vary individually depending on the type of relationships we have. There are several categories of relationships: marriage, friendship, partnership, associate, client, and customer, to name a few. Each type of relationship automatically has its own place of importance in our life. Relational characteristics are exhibited in some social situations and are not appropriate in others. These characteristics may help to define and clarify the importance of that relationship in a person's life.

There are boundaries that we do not cross within each type of relationship. We evaluate our course of action according to each of these specific relationships. Would we place the same importance on someone we consider a stranger versus someone we consider an intimate partner? For example, if we met the president of the United States, would we speak or behave the same as if we invited our friends over to watch a football game? Can we compare our relationship with the president with that of our friends? Do we say both are equal? Would we talk to the president about how we cut ourselves shaving or complain about the yapping dog next door? We probably would not. However, we might tell the president that the economy in our city has seen a recent boom.

What we value in life reveals our priorities. What is important to us? What process do we use to determine the value of something? What values do we engage in order to outline our judgments and opinions? Do we have a set of core beliefs in certain areas? Do we have a consistent pattern we use to conclude our moral views? Or what value is it to own the whole world and do nothing significant with our lives and to have no impact on anyone else's life? What good is it? Do our lives have lasting value? What are we here for? What are our legacies? Our core values are the foundation of life. We must take the time to ask ourselves questions that will help us determine our core belief system. Without a belief system, we will not be building upon a proper foundation. The questions to follow will not have a solid footing if our belief system is not firmly in place.

THE BRIDGE

Some may ask what the outbreak of terrorism today has in common with the teachings of Jesus. The life of Jesus foreshadowed the outbreak of terrorism. Political unrest was the setting of the New Testament and the backdrop for its writings. Many situations faced by biblical characters are no different from troubles throughout our modern world today.

The persecutions of the first-century Christians under Roman oppression and the attacks of Titus in 70 A.D. caused the new believers to truly question their beliefs. Christians faced treason for pronouncing Christ as Lord because to do so would bring into question one's loyalty to Caesar and the Roman government. Many Christians were burned, fed to lions, or forced to fight gladiators in Rome's sports arenas. These terrorist acts affected their economy, security, and most importantly, their core life values. The world has witnessed terrorism throughout the ages. The names and dates are different, but the concept is the same. Can we see the patterns in history that have been repeated throughout time?

Like the Christians in the early Church, people today are faced with new challenges. Are these challenges chiseling in our hearts a new set of values? What are these new values, and how do these values affect us? With these issues facing us, do we have a new perspective on life? What changes, if any, will we make in our lives? Terrorism showcased and brought to the forefront a new set of values to Western thinkers. Is it permissible to take innocent lives for a political or religious cause? What value do we place on life and its importance as we face new challenges? Will the reality of terrorism harden our hearts?

THE QUESTIONS

Jesus was always interested in the heart of any matter. He wanted to know what was most important to a person. What was the heart's motivation behind an action? On one particular day, Jesus spoke with the religious leaders of his day. They were called Pharisees. They criticized him because he healed someone on the Sabbath, a Jewish holy day. They emphasized the significance of certain laws that had been handed down through religious tradition. The Pharisees pointed those laws out to Jesus, insinuating that he had behaved out of order. Jesus, of course, being Jewish, knew these religious laws well. In fact, he had taught in the synagogues where many of these traditions and laws were handed down. However, on this occasion, Jesus simply asked them two questions: **"What man is there among you who has one sheep, and if it falls into a pit on the Sabbath, will not lay hold of it and lift it out?"** (Matt 12:11; Luke 14:5).

A contemporary parallel with Jesus's question might be to compare the beast to our car. If it happened that on a holy day our car was stuck in the mud, a contemporary religious leader would grant us permission to push it out of the mud. This situation would be resolved as a matter of practicality. Jesus's question was piercing and designed to expose religious hypocrisy. Is an animal of more value than a human being? Today he might ask if a vehicle is more important than a person is. His question was asked to provoke them into seeing the bigger picture and to make them define their priorities.

Jesus told a parable about a man who had great possessions. He put them in a barn, filled it to the top, and then asked himself a question: **"And he thought within himself, saying, 'What shall I do, since I have no room to store my crops?'"** (Luke 12:17). This problem confounded him. He had such a large amount that he did not know what to do with it all. Jesus ends this parable by saying the man built a bigger barn and that same night he died.

There are many people in America and around the world who have more belongings than they have space to put the stuff. We hold garage sales to dispose of our excess and sell these belongings for a fraction of the price that we originally paid. We work long hours to earn money only to spend it shopping for things that we might not really need. Where are we going to put it once we buy it?

When Jesus told this parable, he was also speaking to us. This rich man made a decision. He built another barn to accommodate his excess, only to die immediately after finishing his unnecessary endeavor. What value was it to build the barn only to die and not be able to take it with him? What do we do with what is valuable to us? How do we invest it? How do we reconcile it to the whole purpose of our life? Is there a way we can develop our own value system? What makes us happy? Is it jewelry, cars, money, relationships? How long will the temporary euphoria of materialism last? What happens when the happiness wears out? What are the values that are long lasting? Our values will determine how we invest our life.

On another occasion, Jesus asked a unique question: **"And if you do good to those who do good to you, what credit is that to you?"** (Luke 6:33). What value is it to do well by someone only because the same can be expected in return? What is to gain in that? Are our decisions based on what we get in return, or is there some intrinsic value in just doing good for someone who cannot return the favor?

He continued to talk about values by saying, "*. . . you are of more value than many sparrows*" (Luke 12:7). Sparrows could be purchased for pennies on the dollar when Jesus made this statement (See chapter 6, "Spiritual Provisions"). He understood that God is aware of the condition of every sparrow, and Jesus was trying to help people see that they were far more valuable than a common bird. It may be a good idea to look at values from a diverse perspective.

For instance, let's make a contemporary comparison with the use of religious financial practices. Some churches and religious organizations set themselves up as 501(C)3 businesses. The people who give donations to these organizations can receive tax deductions. Some people invest in certain capital investments in which the government offers tax relief. Wouldn't our motivation for placing our resources into the investment be directly related to its return? Is that the value system that Jesus was implying when he asked these questions? He was implying that people are more important in God's view of things than materialism. He really is not talking about doing something *for* his heavenly Father, but he's talking about doing things *with* his Father, as a partner. It is experiencing the value of a relationship with God or with someone else.

Jesus once asked: **"For what profit is it to a man if he gains the whole world, and loses his own soul? Or what will a man give in exchange for his soul?"** (Matt 16:26; Mark 8:36–37; Luke 9:25). What would happen if we gained total domination of everything around us, but when we died, we never went to that heavenly eternal dwelling place? What if we went somewhere else, a place some call "hell," a place of eternal damnation, bitterness, and destruction? Maybe we don't believe in hell or think it is possible that a loving, compassionate God would reject us. But what if we couldn't define God by our own perspective?

He was placing his finger on the core issues of life and death. How does our view of eternity fit within our value system? Some believe that when a person dies, it is the end. Simple annihilation! They have no view of an eternal state or an afterlife. But in a man's last breath would he be able to look back upon his life and say it had any value? Is there life after death, or is it all emptiness? If we knew there was life after death, would we live our lives differently?

On another occasion, Jesus made a statement to the Pharisees. They were teaching the people that if they swore oaths by the temple, it meant nothing, but if anyone would swear by the gold of the temple, he would be bound by his oath. The Pharisees had it backwards, and Jesus was astounded. He asked them, **"For which is greater, the gold or the temple that sanctifies the gold?"** (Matt 23:17). He wanted them to investigate the value of the temple. Was it the material substance that constructed the temple or the temple itself that was more important? God wanted the temple's interior to be ornate because it glorified him. Jesus was asking if the ornate substance of which the temple was made had a more important value than the temple itself. The temple was the center of life for the Jews, and its original purpose was to give life to people as a place to worship the one true God. Jesus was asking them a question to help them evaluate the purpose of the temple. It was a life-giving place where people gathered, not just an ornately decorated building.

Jesus asked questions that would make his audience think about their actions and reactions to everyday life. One subject matter was anxiety. The questions he asked concerned things that people worry about every day, both then and now. He asked a question that is still as remarkable today as it was back then: **"Is not life more than food and the body more than clothing?"** (Matt 6:25). Although anxiety has many faces, its insidious core transcends situation and time. It is a purely negative force, a detriment oppressive to spirit and life. It muddles values, just as it did in Jesus's time. Ours is a materialistic society, replete with oversized SUVs, homes, and wealth. But is the material debt we have accrued equivalent to our spiritual bankruptcy? Is it worthwhile to be anxious about material things that ultimately have no purpose or importance whatsoever? Whenever we are in a stressful situation, it helps to put it into perspective. What will this mean one hundred years from now? Who will remember it ten days from now? If certain things cause us incredible anxiety and harm, it is time to stop and ask ourselves some questions. Do these things carry any lasting spiritual significance? Are they really worth being set back by the anxiety that they cause?

Jesus presented another parable about the priority of values. He asked, **"Or what woman, having ten silver coins, if she loses one coin, does not light a lamp, sweep the house, and search carefully until she finds it?"** (Luke 15:8). Jesus was talking about a concept called the realm of the Kingdom of Heaven. He said the Kingdom is like this woman searching for her coin. She gave it her all, seeking diligently. The emphasis was on the perspective that his Father in heaven was placing on certain values. The effort that would go into finding our lost coin, even greater, the last coin, would be very strenuous. We are going to sweep the whole house and do whatever else we can do to find it. Jesus was trying to emphasize our spiritual priorities and provide a contrast between the spiritual realm and the materialistic realm.

Jesus gave another example while addressing the leaders of that day when he asked, **"What do you think? If a man has a hundred sheep, and one of them goes astray, does he not leave the ninety-nine and go to the mountains to seek the one that is straying?"** (Matt 18:12). The setting in this story is crucial. Jesus was associating himself with those lost in society, such as prostitutes, drunkards, tax collectors, and others who, in his day and ours, are overlooked. He addressed the crowds while confronting the religious leaders. His question was a good one. Is Jesus challenging our values and hypocrisy in relationships just as he was with the Pharisees?

To some, the social status of a person is everything. While many are too busy or oblivious to the needs of those who are hurting, God is pursuing them. Those who are hurting and who are in need will get God's attention. Is that not a clear definition of value? The questions above have a real message. Jesus is speaking to us in everyday terms, using animals and landowners to relate to the value of seeking the Kingdom of Heaven. God has a value for the hurting and insignificant person we may never notice.

In another instance, a rich young man referred to Jesus as a good teacher. By making this statement, this young entrepreneur was attempting to put an appraisal value on Him. Jesus inquired of the wealthy ruler: **"Why do you call Me good?"** (Luke 18:19). Jesus was probing, asking him if he felt he could define Jesus, if he could place a tangible value on Jesus by calling him "good." The first point of emphasis was definition. Did this rich man know what good was? Was he aware of the values necessary to achieve goodness? Did this man even know what he was saying?

Is it possible to define "good" today? Is it a different meaning now than in Jesus's time? What is "good" for us? What is meaningful? What has deep importance to us? Jesus answered the question by saying that only the Father in heaven is good. God alone defines and exemplifies complete goodness. "Good" is not simply what we see and what we want all the time. What is most important, Jesus said, is what the Father of the Kingdom establishes as good.

Jesus again illustrated another set of values. This parable was of a nobleman who went to a far country and left servants to operate his business until he returned. Each one had been given certain talents. It is interesting to observe that money and talents are used to define currency. When the nobleman returned, some had performed well, returning an amount more than they were entrusted with. They were profitable. One worker did nothing but bury (invest) his money in the ground, as he was in fear of the owner.

Jesus, through the parable, asked this question of the man who buried his talent: **"Why then did you not put my money**

in the bank, that at my coming I might have collected it with interest?" (Luke 19:23). This man did nothing with the talent he received. Yet, unaware to himself, he was actually defining his values. The man did not correctly see the value in what he received, so he did not utilize it efficiently. If we do not see value in something, we cannot use it successfully. It will not mean anything, therefore it cannot be used. This man did not recognize, and thus could not utilize, the value of what was given him.

Jesus may be giving us a spiritual principle showing that we all have talents, and these talents are valuable. We all have a destiny, we all have something to offer mankind—talents that are good for the Kingdom and good for other people. We all have unique abilities that God has given us. Jesus is asking us: why we aren't using them? If we are not using them, they do not have any value to us. Why are they not effectively at work in our life? In fact, if our talents are not used, they may be destructive or worse, lost.

When entrepreneurs see the value of something, they take the risk to invest in it. Investors hope to multiply the value of their investment many times over. Their ability to see the value in something is crucial. If it were not for investors, there would be no capitalists, no commerce, no capital profits, no employees, and thus no need for a monetary value system whatsoever.

Many large corporations today determine a CEO's salary as four hundred times the average wage rate. It used to be forty times the average wage thirty years ago. Corporate leaders are taking home hundreds of millions of dollars, in part because they determine the value of the corporation as relative to how much they can take out. What are they going to do with all that money? Is the value system determined by what the employees get? What they feel? What they sense is important?

Jesus once healed ten lepers. They went away, yet one foreigner came back and gave glory to Jesus and to God for healing him. Jesus asked, **"Were there not ten cleansed? But where are** the nine? Were there not any found who returned to give glory to God except this foreigner?" (Luke 17:17–18). Someone who was not part of the system, was not part of the nation, came back and expressed his appreciation because he saw value in what God did for him. The value system of the other nine was based on what they were able to attain from the relationship. Their actions were skewed toward ego and self-preservation rather than the values of gratitude and giving back.

Many of these same questions can be asked of ourselves today. How do we define our values? How can we re-evaluate them and make readjustments? If we discover that we need to re-evaluate our lives, would rearranging our values change the way we live and what we do? Is there a meaningful spiritual value to life that is eternal? Can we investigate it? Can we question ourselves? Jesus asked these questions two thousand years ago, along with many more than we have listed here. Is our life defined by our values? Do we live haphazardly with no direction and purpose beyond the moment? Have we defined those values?

Remember, this book is written about the questions that Jesus asked concerning one realm, one complete designation of life called the Kingdom. He called it the Kingdom of Heaven. There were certain value systems, priorities, and aspects of this realm that he called the Kingdom, which relegated a different lifestyle, a different way of operation. Jesus summarized this whole issue of values in a profound statement: *"But seek first the kingdom of God and His righteousness and all these things shall be added to you"* (Matt 6:33). In other words, trust that there is a perfect value system in this Kingdom. There are priorities. If we seek the Kingdom, search for values in line with the Kingdom, and make them applicable to our life, then all other values that we feel are important to us will fall into place. The *spiritual values* of the Kingdom, which are manifested through our relationships with others, determine the conduct of our lives. When we say he or she had a good life, we need to ask the question that is a paraphrase of the one Jesus asked the wealthy ruler: "How do we determine what is good?"

2

Spiritual Life

The Essence of Living

THE DEFINITION

Life: That property or quality of plants and animals that distinguishes them from inorganic matter or dead organisms; a living being, especially human beings; the existence of the soul; the period of flourishing usefulness.

WEBSTER'S NEW WORLD DICTIONARY

WHAT IS life? How do we find the purpose of life? Does life carry a true purpose or contain an eternal value? Life must be reproduced in order for it to be sustained. When reproduction ceases, stagnancy and ultimately death occur. When we enter a city, do we feel a weighty, oppressive spirit? Or does the city have a vibrant, energetic spirit that is infectious to its people? If we go to into a church, can we determine if life is being produced within? Is there hope? Is a positive, growing spirit prevalent? Most assuredly, in every form of organization it can be ascertained whether life is being produced and sustained.

In many companies, a notion of vitality is real. People scurry around with a sense of urgency. Employees will gather with a certain amount of energy involved. The balance of powers keeps different people in check. Healthy squabbles may arise between departments. For example, the marketing department may feel the factory is not producing enough, and the factory may say that marketing is selling for too low a price. There is a sense of tension but also a sense of life. Innovations continually come over the horizon, bringing new products. There is a vision, and the company grows and reproduces itself. It starts other plants, outposts, and distributorships. It is the same way with schools, families, churches, and other social institutions. They produce either life or death. In a healthy residential community, roads and houses are maintained and expanded, with new amenities being developed. In the housing market, there is a difference between a depressed area and one that is flourishing, with new houses and people moving in.

THE BRIDGE

An important objective of this book is to describe spiritual life and to demonstrate Jesus's approach to the meaning of life. Jesus always used a comparison between the kingdom of the world and the Kingdom of Heaven. He used parables to describe and explain life in his time and in ours. He told us how life could be most effective and enjoyable. He taught how to reproduce the joy of life. He communicated through questions the essence and vitality of the Kingdom of God.

Through these questions, Jesus reflected a comparison and contrast to the religious system of that day. He compared life of the Kingdom to the alternative—the destructive force of evil, which leads to death. Most of what Jesus talked about drew a definitive line between one form of activity and another. One group would produce life, and one group would produce death. There was always a definitive comparison between the two. There was always a contrast. He had a problem with the religious system, partially because of the rules, regulations, and ritualism that existed within it. A strict sense of legalism corrupted God's law and began to bring death by stifling the spirit of God's word. Jesus came to free individuals from bondage, emptiness, and helplessness. He thus exposed the corrosive aspects of religion in comparison to the life that the Kingdom produces. It was a brand new way of portraying what God the Creator was all about.

THE QUESTIONS

Jesus asked the Pharisees a critical question: **"How then will his kingdom stand?"** (Matt 12:26). It is the imperative question of his time and ours. Jesus had cast out a demon, and the Pharisees claimed it to be the work of Satan. This claim suggested that the life-affirming miracles Jesus performed were generated from the negative power of Satan. Jesus thus explained that any form of organization that is divided internally ultimately will crumble. He asked, **"If Satan also is divided against himself, how will his kingdom stand?"** (Luke 11:18). If Satan expelled his own demons, he would be weakening himself. Further, Jesus was challenging them to show how his miracles, which produced life, could be interpreted as being born of evil.

This incident sparked a debate amongst the religious leaders concerning what Jesus was doing in regard to the Kingdom. The religious systems, composed partially of the Pharisees and Sadducees, were trying to discredit him. They claimed that not only was he not the Messiah, but also that his miracles were born of evil. Jesus's response was very critical. He said that any organization or system divided against itself would not be able to exist very long. If a system is divided against itself, it is fragmented and headed for destruction. If it is not united, it loses value, purpose, and direction. It has no reproductive power and thus does not have life.

He continued, **"And if I cast out demons by Beelzebub, by whom do your sons cast them out?"** (Matt 12:27; Luke 11:19).

He was implying that no organization could long stand if it comes against itself. How could the Pharisees accuse Jesus of bringing death when he so obviously brought new life to the demon-possessed man? If they agreed with Jesus that Satan's kingdom could not stand if divided, they would have no choice but to acknowledge the presence of the Kingdom of God inherent in the life-producing actions of Jesus. This is crucial to the issue of producing and reproducing life. If there is division, nothing will work. Jesus said later, *"He who is not with Me is against Me, and he who does not gather with Me scatters"* (Luke 11:23). In other words, when we come together and develop a spirit of unity, we produce life. When we remain isolated and fragmented spiritually, we become scattered, and death results.

There are situations that seem to be life producing on the surface. Some families may appear strong when actually, a life-producing spiritual connection is absent, and they end up fragmented by divorce. Many churches have functions that seem to be alive but are not. Jesus cited an example of this in the book of Revelation, when he stated: *"I know your deeds; you have a reputation of being alive, but you are dead"* (Rev 3:1, NIV). Life always has a redeeming value. It has a unifying function. There is productivity and a cohesive strength. A good sports team has a unifying purpose. If there is a spirit of division or competition of egos within the team, the team will not achieve long-term success. Jesus said that life is about working together, being of one purpose, and being connected with integrity and character. Life is defined by how well we work together, remain congruent, and have a teamwork approach to every endeavor we take on, especially in the area of the Kingdom.

Imagine being amongst a crowd, following Jesus, listening to him and watching him perform miracles. He asks, **"Or else how can one enter a strong man's house and plunder his goods, unless he first binds the strong man?"** (Matt 12:29). Then and now his analogous questions provoke more questions. The mysterious artistry of Jesus's questions is amazing. He switched gears frequently. He took authority through the power of the interrogative, asking intriguing and provocative questions designed to prod his audience toward his grand goal. We cannot reverse the dynamics of those things that are not of God without having the strength and authority to take hold of it and bind it up. We must trust God's will and be empowered with resolve and such absoluteness that it completely restructures the entire situation. We have to resist Satan and everything pertaining to him (1 Pet 5:8–9). Jesus has asked his people to empower themselves through him to confront Satan. He is equipping us with the strength to do his will.

God's ability to emancipate a person, city, or nation and bring life is profound. The power of God is an emancipating power. It has the capability to deliver from oppressive forces and completely dissipate them. When Satan enters a community, he does the same thing. He binds up the strength of that area and causes it to become ineffective. He dilutes the power of protection over family, church, and community, thus draining it of life. When Jesus asked the question regarding the strongman, he was really asking the religious system of his day. Likewise, we can bring revival to a spiritually arid city. We know that redemption and renewal will follow when God's life is present. Any nation that submits itself to the power of God begins to be set free, to be productive, and to flourish. Only God can achieve this through the people that he chooses to carry out his plans. There are, however, repercussions involved, often in the form of persecution. A true emancipator is often persecuted by those whom he came to deliver, which is exactly what happened to Jesus! He came to deliver his nation and was crucified for it, but in the end, he set the world free and gave us life!

In this same conversation with the Pharisees, Jesus made clear the nature of their hearts when he asked them, "**How can you, being evil, speak good things?**" (Matt 12:34). The implication Jesus made is that nothing life giving can come from anything that is inherently bad. A person with faulty or destructive motives cannot produce life, but persons and things that are full of life will always produce life. There is no middle ground. Life produces fruit. This is the positive message of the Kingdom of God. The gospel is not a list of do's and don'ts. It is God's word, a tool of empowerment meant to set the heart full of life.

Life-givers always threaten those who are life-takers. Those who are greedy for power and have faulty motives always resist life-givers. Fort Pierce is a city on the east coast of Florida, a city that for a long time was severely oppressed and in dire need of revival. A coalition of business, civic, and church leaders came together to fight for the cause of Christ and biblical values in this city. The crime rate declined, along with racism, and the community united and began to prosper. The whole downtown began to reshape and reform with new streetlights and the renovation of buildings. Businesses began to see the potential for growth in the area. It was a total and complete revival that occurred because of the emancipators who came and utilized their talents.

West Palm Beach, Florida, is another town that has been totally rejuvenated. Previously, areas of West Palm Beach had become run down and dangerous. In the mid 1970s the pastor of First Baptist Church, Jess Moody, brought people of vision together and twenty years later, the entire city was renovated. People can once again walk at night without trepidation. This area is now replete with beautiful restaurants and stores remaining open late into the evening. There are many stories of people who have been emancipated and have hence brought fresh breath into dead situations.

Another dynamic occurred under Jesus's ministry. He fed thousands of people when there was no food to eat. He broke bread and fed the thousands who were following him (Matt 15:32–38). Some time later, He and His followers were on the other side of the lake. He began to discuss being aware of the yeast of the

Pharisees (Matt 16:5-7). He was warning them of the destructive power within the religious system that causes manipulation and bureaucracies. The disciples began to murmur among themselves, not fully understanding his meaning. They thought that maybe he was talking about the bread that they did not take with them when he fed the five thousand. They began to second-guess themselves. Sensing this, he asked them a question. **"O you of little faith. Why do you reason among yourselves because you have brought no bread?"** (Matt 16:8).

Once again, the disciples could not readily discern the true meaning of Jesus's words. He was cautioning them regarding the yeast of the Pharisees, demonstrating how demonic forces can exist within bureaucratic systems. Families, governments, churches, and other institutions become bureaucracies when they gather unto themselves a protective aura that is resistant to any form of change. If change occurs, stability is at least temporarily weakened. Bureaucracy feeds on itself to the extent that the hierarchical systems become stagnant and oppressive and bondage takes hold. Jesus, as a prophet of change, came to emancipate us from bondage and give us life.

Systems do not bring life. Life brings life. Stability and structure are necessary with any organization, but Jesus warned that once the system becomes more important than its cause, it becomes dead. Many church denominations are dying today. They are reducing in numbers. Part of the reason is because the bureaucracy today is the same as that of Jesus's day. The Pharisee system of bureaucracy takes root and does not allow change. Therefore, it becomes dead. In Europe, many beautiful structures were once sanctuaries ministering to thousands of people. Today they are empty monuments. They have very little life in them.

Many times in the gospels, the stories begin with the Pharisees or teachers of the law coming to Jesus for various reasons in various places. One time while in Jerusalem, the Pharisees came up to Jesus and asked him why his disciples broke the tradition of the elders by not washing their hands before eating. Religious tradition required a long ritual of washing, one to which the disciples did not adhere. Jesus did not care about the mere ritual. It was beyond what was needed for hygienic purposes. It was just something that the bureaucracy had established at the time. Jesus asked questions to deal with the hypocrisy: **"Are you also still without understanding? Do you not yet understand that whatever enters the mouth goes into the stomach and is eliminated?"** (Matt 15:16–17; Mark 7:18).

He challenged them by asking if they understood. Later on, he would ask them if they were still so dull. Eighteen times Jesus asked in the gospels, "Do you understand?" He was like a coach or father, imploring us toward comprehension. Jesus wanted everyone to stop and think for a moment, and after empowering them to do so, he asked if his meaning was understood. He was explaining how the people of the religious system could perform its rituals, go to church, follow all sorts of regulations, and expand on them. However, none of this as such will create a person who produces life for the Kingdom unless the motives of the heart are correct. The ability to produce life is determined by eternal values that are Kingdom of Heaven empowered.

What determines if we are clean or unclean is the life or death within us. Sexual immoralities, theft, murder, and other forms of evil rise from the hardness and self-centeredness of the heart. Jesus was telling the religious leaders that none of their man-made traditions, their laws and rituals, could reverse the evil inherent in them. Elsewhere, Jesus said, *". . . For out of the abundance of the heart, the mouth speaks"* (Matt 12:34). Out of the mouth, either life or death is produced. Health is produced. The fruit of the spirit of love, joy, patience, and other things that help people and give a sense of purpose all flow from the abundance of a good heart, not rules and regulations; not what we eat or the ritual we have with it.

Another question came when Jesus was about to suffer on the cross. It was the time when Simon of Cyrene was about to take up Jesus's cross to help him. Jesus could hear the women wailing as he was taking his cross up to Calvary. They were crying and weeping. He turned to these women and said, **"For if they do these things in the green wood, what will be done in the dry?"** (Luke 23:31). He was questioning how much worse things could become once he had returned to heaven. He was healing those in need, bringing life and joy, setting hearts free, and pouring love into people. In return, he was crucified. Knowing his final hour was at hand, Jesus rhetorically asked the wailing women what would become of the world once he left and the end comes. Even today, Christianity's influence is not what it was fifty years ago. Jesus said that in the last days, hearts would wax cold and even the elect would be deceived. The time he predicts will be a time when life is no longer spiritually oriented. This time will be oriented to the world. There will be an emphasis instead on material goods and other desires not related to his Kingdom.

Looking at the ever-increasing breakup of families and the moral decay of our nation, it is obvious that the impact of church on society is dwindling. Today, the notion of homosexuals marrying and raising children and having the same rights as married people is steadily gaining acceptance in the world. It is an accepted matter of law in Canada. This is an aberration that fifty years ago would not have even been considered. We live in what many refer to as "The New Age." This New Age is spiritually dry. It is not life giving, and it is going to produce death. Jesus acknowledges as much through his question to the wailing women, wondering how much lower man's heart could sink.

Another time, Jesus asked, **"Which of you by worrying can add one cubit to his stature?"** (Matt 6:27; Luke 12:25). **"If you then are not able to do the least, why are you anxious for the rest?"** (Luke 12:26). What defines our priorities in regard to life? We need to ask ourselves, "What produces life? Is it material things like cars and houses?" There are majestic houses, castles, and beautiful mansions that have no life in them whatsoever. Jesus wondered why we worry about anything that cannot add any spiritual value or length to our lives. There are far more pertinent issues to consider than what we own, what we are going to wear, or what we are going to eat tomorrow.

He asked, **"So why do you worry about clothing?"** (Matt 6:28). Yet, that is the force behind what many identify as life, whether they have the right clothes or two cars or a beautiful home with a perfect lawn. It is a sad day when those values, those things that we call life, are most important to us. Jesus tells us that worry can only bring anxiety and death. If we do not trust in what God wants for us and what he is willing to supply to us, we are in trouble. Life is not being produced or duplicated in us.

Terrorism has recently become one of America's greatest threats. Reports of it are constant in the news media. Since September 11, 2001, a fear lingers that someone can blow up another building or institution at any time. Fear is a great hindrance to life. We cannot seem to stop it, because we do not know where it is going to pop up. It is like lightning or a tornado. We don't know when it is going to happen. When we are anxious, life is taken from us. When we worry about the security of our job, or our financial future, and trust the world's system for the things that we need, we fail to accomplish the goal that God sets for us. His plan for us is not about those things. It is about producing the fruit of the Spirit. These are intangible qualities.

Jesus uniquely compared the forces of life and the forces of death. Neither kingdom can stand divided. There needs to be a unified and compelling force to make any entity come to bear fruit. Death produces death, and life produces life. Jesus asked, **"Do you not understand this parable? How then will you understand all the parables?"** (Mark 4:13). He told a story about a farmer sowing seed along the road, on rocky soil, among the thorn bushes, and onto fertile ground. He compared these four places that the farmer sows seed (Mark 4:3–8). When Jesus told this parable about the fruit that came from these plantings, the disciples again could not understand the meaning behind the story. *He implied in the above questions that if they could not understand this story, then they could not understand all the other stories he told.*

His point was that any endeavor not of the Lord ultimately would lead to futility. It will be ineffective and produce nothing. If we plant in the rocky soil where there is little fertility, it will produce for a short period, but it cannot take root. Life is not produced in those areas. Plant amongst the bushes and there might be growth to some degree. However, the bushes represent the cares of the world, and they will eventually block growth of faith. Life will not be able to flourish. Jesus then talked about the seed sown on fertile ground. He urged us to sow our seeds of faith and life in a place of fertility that will bring forth fruit. They will be watered and grow and their roots will reach deep into the soil and produce exponentially. Jesus was telling us that this parable was the key to all his stories about life, what makes life fruitful, and what makes life multiply.

Jesus asked, **"To what shall we liken the kingdom of God? Or with what parable shall we picture it?"** (Mark 4:30; Luke 13:18, 20). Jesus answered his own questions by comparing faith to a tiny mustard seed. The mustard seed is one of the smallest of seeds, yet it grows into a great tree. A small amount of *spiritual life* used properly can impact communities, families, and nations. Jesus is a life giver, a Kingdom producer. We may look at our faith as a mustard seed—very small and insignificant—but with Jesus it can grow, blossom, and produce everlasting fruit wherever we go. This fruit of the Spirit is the essence of life.

3

Spiritual Relationships

The Heart of the Church

THE DEFINITION

Relationship: The quality or state of being related; connected; connection by blood, marriage, etc.; kinship; a particular instance of being related.

Webster's New World Dictionary

Jesus was deeply concerned with relationships. In the modern church, there are major concerns, such as ministries, budgets, and attendance. However, these issues were not of primary concern with Jesus. He talked about relating to each other and to his Father in heaven. Jesus said that we would be known by our fruit. He did not say we would be known by the size of our church or even for how many were saved under its ministry. How do we relate to others? What kind of people are we? What is our character? Is the fruit of the Spirit evident in our lives to the point that we positively influence others? This is our legacy. The reason we exist, Jesus proclaimed, is to relate to others and to him. It is imperatively the number one purpose of our life. We cannot function effectively without relationships.

This seems to be the message Jesus was communicating when he asked a series of questions pertaining to relationships. Most of the chapters in this book reflect questions that were asked to the religious system of Jesus's day. People gathered to listen to these questions and interchanges. Imagine it is two thousand years ago and pretend that we are standing in the crowd or in the porticos of the temple or on the streets or in a house somewhere. Maybe someone from the religious system came up to Jesus and challenged his actions or words. Perhaps Jesus was with his disciples clarifying a parable or situation for them. It was in this context that Jesus asked many questions concerning motives and relationships. These questions were designed to elicit truth and growth in his disciples, and in us.

THE BRIDGE

Perhaps Jesus is speaking to us today through these questions. He may be questioning the church today. Has it lost its priority on relationships? We have all kinds of programs and books that address how to grow a church and how to make ministry more effective. But are the leaders of the church demonstrating how to build an effective body of people? Do they have people around them who are capable of showing the rest of the body of Christ how to build strong spiritual relationships? This is rarely seen in churches today. Mostly we see mechanics or great performances. We see wonderful teaching and preaching. We see structure and system—all of which can help increase attendance. We have made attendance the emphasis on church development. How many people go to our church? How many ministries do we have? What is our budget?

These are not issues that are of much concern to Jesus. What really matters to him, aside from our faith, is how we relate to one another. Today we have megachurches, yet we see our country in moral decay. Relationships are falling apart. The basic interpersonal relational aspects upon which Jesus focused are now deteriorating. There is a host of negative influences eager to derail us from building solid spiritual relationships. Our megachurches and rejoicing Sunday morning mentality appears ideal in our competitive society, but these values can conflict with what Jesus taught. He spoke of and asked questions pertaining to the Kingdom of God, family life, and the way we treat one another.

Early in the book of Acts, we read that Jesus's believers met together daily and went from house to house. There was no formal "church" yet, only followers of Jesus who believed in him as a community. These followers gathered together daily in the porticos of the temple. They followed "the apostles' teaching." They broke bread together. They sold their possessions in order to provide for those in need. This reflects a completely different scenario than what we see today in the church. We do not see pastors exchanging pulpits in the same city. We do not see numbers added daily to the fellowships. The typical Sunday morning church service today features one person standing up and preaching for an hour, and afterward everyone goes home. That is the emphasis on church activity today. When people say that they go to church, that means they go to a building, sing some songs, and listen to someone speak and go home. The model that we see today does not reflect the biblical model of what the church should look like.

What we see in many churches today is not geared to family ministry. There are major efforts in many churches to promote fellowship groups and home groups. This is good because it gives people an opportunity to come together. Although in many cases, the system of fellowship groups and the growth aspect of these groups become more important than why we are fellowshipping. So, as with many other movements in the past, the method becomes more important than the reason the method exists. It is all about growth, all about being big. People get into this system and thus become proponents of it. They connect themselves with it, but they are relying on the system to make the church function rather than developing intimate and close relationships with each other and with God.

THE QUESTIONS

In the Beatitudes, Jesus asked, **"And if you greet your brethren only, what do you do more than others? Do not even the tax collectors do so?"** (Matt 5:47). This question is a pointed measure of our engagement with others. Isn't it true that those we have developed relationships with are the ones we normally talk to? We greet them, pay attention to them, and favor them. But those we don't know, those who are strangers, we very rarely open up to, embrace, or try to get to know. In fact, there is no ready environment in most churches in which people can get to know one another. Instead, people sit in rows and look at the back of each other's heads. We need to learn how to engage others, but we are not taught. We are not taught how to care about someone we do not know. We could be going to the same church for years and have the same hundred people sitting around us every Sunday but never develop any kind of relationship with them. We must learn to focus energy into engaging people outside our network of friends. This is exactly what Jesus was imploring us to do by asking the question above.

Jesus told us in Matthew 5:48 to be perfect like our heavenly Father. God reaches out to everyone. Relationship building is not sitting in church, listening to someone preach for an hour, listening to some music, and going home. This is not what God intended for his church. If we only develop relationships with those who can benefit us, we are behaving no differently than the world does. There is no paradigm change. Jesus urged us to have a positive impact on our culture, rather than letting it dictate our actions and behavior. He wants us to affect our culture instead of being affected by it. We need to encourage ourselves to escape our comfort zone, take risks, and as leaders, begin to address the issue of fragmented relationships.

Matthew 25 records a section where Jesus spoke about the last days and the return of the Son of Man. Jesus talked about his Kingdom and about us receiving an inheritance in his Kingdom from the Father in heaven. He said that those who receive this inheritance would be greatly blessed. In the middle of this dialogue, Jesus asked questions in a story that will be asked of him in those last days: **"Then the righteous will answer Him, saying, 'Lord, when did we see You hungry and feed You, or thirsty and give You drink? When did we see You a stranger and take You in, or naked and clothe You? Or when did we see You sick, or in prison, and come to You?'"** (Matt 25:37–39). This is the same question that the disciples around him would have asked him. Jesus finished the story by answering his own questions, stating, *"Assuredly, I say to you, inasmuch as you did it to one of the least of these My brethren, you did it to Me."* (Matt 25:40). Jesus asked and answered the question. He created a question to answer the question. How does our Lord get blessed? It is through relationships, through people exerting an effort to bless someone else to help someone into a better position than where he or she was before.

Righteousness, according to Jesus, is determined by the conduct of our relationship with those who are not significant, helping those around us who are unnoticed. At Dunklin Camp, a ministry led by Mickey Evans west of Stuart, Florida, there are pictures of many saints with a sign proclaiming them as "Jewels from the Devil's Junk Pile." These are people, raised up under Mickey's discipleship, who are producing life in many others. The people who came to Dunklin are society's marginalized. They came broken with addictions and other life-restraining problems. Later in the New Testament, James writes about paying too much attention to the rich, leaving behind those who seem insignificant and needy. This is a very critical issue that Jesus was trying to get across. He truly is blessed by our reaching out to those who cannot help themselves. It is as if we are doing it unto the Lord. He receives it as if it were done for him. It is doing an unrewarded kindness to others that is so important to the Kingdom. The most spiritually rewarding form of living is bonding in relationships with others.

Another interesting question Jesus asked pertains to breaking down fears, racial and cultural prejudices, and various other boundaries that deter us from forming relationships. People came to Jesus about John the Baptist. They were troubled by the image of John. He lived in the wilderness, ate locusts, and wore camel hair, while teaching about the Kingdom of God. He was a very strong personality and preached repentance to even the elite of the day. He also baptized people and spoke words from the Lord. People weren't sure what to make of him. Jesus asked, **"What did you go out into the wilderness to see? A reed shaken by the wind?"** (Matt 11:7; Luke 7:24). Jesus moved into the interrogative and questioned their expectations. He continued, **"But what did you go out to see? A man clothed in soft garments?"** (Matt 11:8; Luke 7:25) **"But what did you go out to see? A prophet?"** (Matt 11:9; Luke 7:26) Jesus wondered what they were looking for when they followed John into the wilderness. He then told them, *"I tell you, among those born of women there is no one greater than John . . ."* (Luke 7:28; NIV). This spoke to the strength of relationship between Jesus and John. John the Baptist was not what the people neither expected nor wanted to see. He didn't have the personality, culture, looks, clothing, or anything else of worldly value. But John was in relationship with Jesus. John believed in Jesus. This belief and faith was priceless in comparison to anything the world could offer.

The church today is in dire need of those who have a relationship with the Lord similar to that of John the Baptist, and who will speak on the Lord's behalf regarding the faltering relationships between and within people and churches. Maybe this person won't look like someone we ought to accept, and maybe he will speak tough words that we do not want to hear. But we will need to hear it, so that our relationships with each other and with the Lord will be what he intended them to be in the Church.

Jesus asked a question that we ought to ask ourselves: "**Who do men say that I, the Son of Man, am?**" (Matt 16:13). Two verses later he asked, "**But who do you say that I am?**" (Matt 16:15). What a pointed question! Jesus already knew what people thought about him, but he felt it was important to ask the question so that Peter and others might express their answer. It's a question that we ought to be cognizant of in the Church. We who are in the Church as part of the Church probably need to ask ourselves some questions: Who is Jesus? Who do people say that we are? How does the world look at us? What is its opinion of us? What kind of impact do we have on it? What kind of relationship do we have outside our sphere of influence? What kind of answer would we get? Would people see us as a threateningly extreme right-wing organization? Would they call us fundamentalists? Or would they consider us as people who care and nurture? Would they see a unified people with one belief system? We might be well served to ask ourselves in the Church what sort of response to these questions we might illicit and deserve.

Jesus became vulnerable when he asked that question: how do you see me? Isn't that a great question for pastors, teachers, evangelists, TV evangelists, and other leaders to ask? How do I appear to you? How am I coming across? It's a good question to ask our spouses, our bosses, our co-workers, and our friends—not only about us individually but about the institution called the Church. Peter answered Jesus's question, proclaiming him as "... the Christ, the Son of the living God" (Matt 16:16). Jesus was doing something right to make such an impression on Peter. Are we as Christians individually and in the church deserving of a positive response in regard to the impression that we create for ourselves? Would people today see the Church as a valid representation of Jesus?

Jesus showed his vulnerability and the personality of the Father in heaven in another question he asked. Jesus turned to the twelve, his closest friends, and said, **"You do not want to leave too, do you?"** (John 6:67; NIV). He asked that question starting in John 6:53 when he spoke of eating his flesh and drinking his blood and partaking of him. It's the fundamental foundation to the communion passage in the Passover and the Last Supper. He was talking about intimacy with him and truly partaking in him through a spiritual experience that would be as close to him as one could get. It is like someone coming to us and putting his or her hand on our shoulder and asking us to be a close friend, to stand by them undoubtedly. A question this direct might give us pause, cause indecisiveness, and make us uncomfortable. It might ultimately cause us to walk away. This was precisely the crowd's reaction to the above question asked by Jesus. They felt awkward and uncomfortable and began to leave. Then he turned to the twelve and asked if they were going to leave him also. This was a painful question. Jesus showed us the Father's pain.

We can ask this question in many of our relationships. Sometimes we go through divorce, family breakups, or business partnership breakups, all of which can create feelings of hurt and betrayal. Relationships can be painful, and the most painful experience we can have is the breaking of a relationship, abandonment, or separation and the deep hurt it causes. Perhaps we are not vulnerable to people because of the pain that can result when we let down our guard.

Jesus was vulnerable. He brought these disciples close to him. He spent three and half years with them and poured his life into them and was willing to be rejected. This is not a very familiar concept today. Usually pastors and leaders of churches are somewhat separated from their congregations, and bonding is increasingly hard to find in many churches. However, this is not always the case. Sometimes smaller churches have very close, intimate relationships. However, when churches start growing and become large, it can become increasingly difficult to develop close, intimate relationships. The whole process that Jesus followed of pouring his life into these men for three and a half years is not common in Church leadership today. We don't see Jesus's life as a template for how to raise up ministry. We go to seminary or to other training and graduate. We are assigned to a certain job or a certain congregation. Good as this may be, how can Church leaders become effective if they have not been discipled as Jesus discipled?

In the dimension of being critical of and in competition with others, Jesus asked this question: **"And why do you look at the speck in your brother's eye, but do not consider the plank in your own eye?"** (Matt 7:3; Luke 6:41). We have heard this many times. Christian and non-Christian alike have often paraphrased this question. Then Jesus asked a second question: **"Or how can you say to your brother, 'Let me remove the speck from your eye'; and look, a plank is in your own eye?"** (Matt 7:4; Luke 6:42). Something inherent in our sinful nature creates in us a desire to outdo others, but are we humble enough to accept our own failings? Where is our humility? The emphasis today seems to be on bigger church buildings, with high attendance as a sure sign of success. It might help reshape our perspective, however, to remember that, after three and one half years of ministry, Jesus only had 120 faithful followers he assigned to the upper room before he ascended to heaven.

There can be many more questions listed here with comments, but as we look at the list in the back of this book, we can see Jesus was most concerned about effective, pure, and transparent relationships. Every word Jesus spoke addressed *spiritual relationships*.

4

Spiritual Alignment

A Discourse on Authoritative Structure

THE DEFINITION

Alignment: (1) (a) an aligning or being aligned; arrangement in a straight line; (b) a condition of close cooperation (a new alignment of European nations); (2) a line or lines formed by aligning; (3) Engineering a ground plan, as of a fieldwork, railroad, etc.

Webster's New World Dictionary

Alignment is a condition whereby various parts come into order. This condition consists of efficient operation and harmony among these various parts. A car aligned properly will run smoothly with no tire wear. Alignment is critical in government, work, church, mechanical apparatuses, and in every other facet of life. Where there is proper alignment, there is order. Discovering and implementing this order helps develop an efficient and well-run organization, machine, or anything else where it is applied. Some believe that there is alignment in the spiritual realm. Others see the universe as a continuing cycle of random occurrences. Most civil minds concur regarding the need for societal containment through laws aimed at preserving order and preventing subversion. However, many disagree over the nature and origin of order. Many argue order comes from the necessary endeavors of humanity to protect itself.

Others believe God created order, aligned the planets, and scripted the physical laws of nature. They believe the spoken word of God created the universe. They do not view the world as random and chaotic. Many see heaven and earth as aligned, planned order in the form of judicial systems and other systems God has ordained. They see God's order manifested in creation, in the rule of law by which we live. They believe our societal laws are rooted in the Ten Commandments established by God, and they live according to other spiritual perspectives written in the Bible.

THE BRIDGE

In the days of Jesus, the Jews had an order and an hierarchical religious system. They did not exactly see the heart of God or accept the true purpose of his temple. The religious system of the time began to exalt itself as the main authority regarding the nation of Israel instead of seeking the will of God first. Therefore, many conflicts occurred between what Jesus taught and what the Pharisees and Sadducees believed.

THE QUESTIONS

Jesus addressed the issue of alignment within the religious system and said things to confront the Sadducees and the Pharisees. He asked the Pharisees, **"What do you think about the Christ? Whose son is He?"** (Matt 22:42). These questions required the Pharisees to face the complex issue of Jesus's Messiahship. These questions confounded and required them to define their spiritual alignment, causing them to ponder the deepest sensitivities of their theology. Jesus continually established his alignment and authority. He questioned the religious system's understanding of God's alignment.

Jesus had another question for the Pharisees: **"How then does David, in the spirit call him 'Lord' saying: the Lord said to my Lord, sit at my right hand till I make your enemies your foot stool?"** (Matt 22:43–44). If Christ were in the lineage of David, why would David call him Lord? According to the Old Testament, David was the greatest king of Israel. This question stumped the Pharisees, and they could not answer it. It was yet another of the many questions Jesus asked for the purpose of inspiring his audience to ponder deeply the significance and meaning of his message. Why did he ask them? What context were they asked in? What is the deeper meaning of what he is asking us to think about today? Oftentimes in the church we elevate our buildings, our performances, our preaching, our personalities, and our ministries. As Jesus asked, however, who is the Son of God? Is he being exalted?

He asked another question: **"If then David calls him 'Lord' how is he the son?"** (Matt 22:45; Mark 12:37; Luke 20:44). The religious leaders of the time wore long robes and prayer shawls, steadfastly followed religious rituals and traditions, and took authority over the people. They mandated bureaucratic religious programs, had great influence and esteem, and were exalted for having religious titles and names. However, Jesus simply asked questions that, despite their religiosity, they could not answer! All of their theology, power, and authority could not help them answer these simple questions. Jesus may have some things for us to think about regarding our alignment as he did two thousand years ago when he talked to the Pharisees.

In the book of Luke, Jesus asked another profound question: **"But why do you call me 'Lord, Lord' and do not do the things which I say?"** (Luke 6:46). This truly is an alignment question! Jesus was speaking to a large crowd, discoursing about loving enemies and judging others. He told a few parables in this discourse, but right in the middle he asked the above question. It is yet another timeless question for us to consider. Are we really doing what Jesus says to do? Are we really following the Sermon on the Mount, the Beatitudes, where he talked about loving enemies and turning the other cheek? Do we love one another to the extent that everybody outside the church knows that we are disciples because of this love? Or are we divided? Are we really in alignment with each other and with the Lord? Are Christian families staying together? Are leaders of our church serving others? Are we washing feet? Or are power relationships being set up where we have titles for our Christian leaders? Are we setting up our own hierarchy? Are we wearing fancy robes and exercising dominion over people in such a way that we exalt ourselves?

Jesus once said, "*Foxes have holes and birds of the air have nests, but the Son of Man has no place to lay his head*" (Matt 8:20; Luke 9:58; NIV). Are we humble? Are our hearts contrite? Are we allowing ourselves to be molded into his image and his character? Jesus is asking us not only to acknowledge and receive him as our Lord and Savior but also to do his will.

Jesus asked a question regarding his alignment with his Father, how he exemplified the character of who he was, and what he wanted us to be (Luke 7:36–39). One of the Pharisees invited Jesus to have dinner with him and others at his home. A certain woman who lived a sinful life in that town learned that Jesus was eating at this Pharisee's home so she brought an alabaster jar of perfume. She kneeled down at Jesus's feet and began wiping them with her tears and with the perfume. The Pharisees, along with the others present, felt that a true prophet would have been able to distinguish the type of sinful woman she was.

Sensing their self-righteous disdain, Jesus asked them a question: **"Do you see this woman?"** (Luke 7:44). Obviously, everyone saw the woman. Why did Jesus ask this question? He knew what everyone was thinking. Jesus was asking if they truly understood her actions. He reminded them that when he came into the Pharisee's home, this Pharisee did not get any water for his feet, did not greet him with a kiss nor put oil on his head, and did not even recognize Jesus as anybody! But this woman wet his feet with her tears, wiped them with her hair, kissed his feet, and put oil on his head! They did not realize that this woman was seeking forgiveness for what she had done and who she was. They were unable to see the heart of this woman. They did not understand that she recognized an alignment that they could not comprehend. They were unable to grasp who Jesus was and what he was about. Jesus could forgive her sins and was able to forgive theirs too! But if they could not recognize who Jesus was, the alignment under which he willingly placed himself, and what God was doing through him, they could not receive what this woman would surely receive.

In the 1970s and early '80s a revival occurred. It was an outpouring of God's Spirit of love for Jesus. Many young people came to the Lord. Many came from outside of any religious or denominational system. It was a demonstration of the love of God. Spiritual songs were written, people were praising the Lord, and God's Spirit was poured out in many ways, causing large numbers of people to depart from the religious system and the denominational churches. Many simple people, like the sinful woman mentioned in the passage above, saw Jesus. People began to shun the notion of hierarchy inherent in many churches, and many began to love and worship Jesus in the same humble spirit as this sinful woman. A refreshing realignment occurred. A whole renewal and outpouring took form. There were extremes in the movement, but the Lord poured out his blessing through it.

In John 10, a dialogue goes on between the Jews who gathered in the Colonnade for a dedication in Jerusalem. It was winter, and the Jews were around the outside of the temple. They were asking about the identity of Jesus. They were concerned about who he was and whether he was who he claimed to be. So, they asked Jesus to tell them if he was the Christ. They wanted him to state it plainly. Jesus instead reminded them of all the miracles he performed in the name of his heavenly Father. These miracles ought to have spoken volumes about who he was, but they nonetheless stood fast in their unbelief because they could not recognize his alignment with God. They were unwilling to accept him as the Messiah and had not recognized him as the Son of God in spite of all he accomplished.

Jesus then made a provocative statement to the Jews: "*I and the Father are One*" (John 10:30; NIV). Jesus was forthright and clear in declaring his perfect alignment with God. If we say that we are one with the Father, then we are right where we are supposed to be, doing what we are supposed to be doing. This declaration infuriated his audience. The Jews considered this declaration as heresy, so they prepared to stone him. Jesus, referring to his many miracles, asked, "**For which of those works do you stone me?**" (John 10:32). Jesus was questioning their motives for hating him as they did. Was it because they did not believe he really was in alignment with God? Did they wholeheartedly disagree with everything he said? Or was it because of the miracles he performed in God's name? The Jews answered that they were preparing to stone him because he claimed to be God! He claimed absolute alignment with the heavenly Father, the Creator of the universe, the I Am, Yahweh! He claimed that he and God were one (John 10:30)!

Jesus then began to ask another series of questions. He asked, "**Is it not written in your law, 'I said you are gods?' If he called them gods to whom the word of God came (and the Scripture cannot be broken), do you say of him whom the Father sanctified, and sent into the world, 'You are blaspheming,' because I said, 'I am the Son of God?'**" (John 10:34–36) There is a reference in the Old Testament that Jesus used from Psalm 82. If Jesus performed miracles, why did the Jews want to stone him for claiming to be the Son of God? Jesus was urging them at least to believe in his miraculous acts that they witnessed, even if they refused to believe in him. Jesus stated, "*That you may know and understand that the Father is in Me and I in the Father*" (John 10:38; NIV). Jesus was telling them that if they could not trust his words, they could trust what their own eyes had seen him do. How could the Old Testament call some "gods" and yet criticize Jesus for saying he was the Son of God?

Here is another example of Jesus knowing his alignment. Jesus was in the Garden of Gethsemane when the guards came to arrest him and take him before Pilate. One of Jesus's companions, Peter, reached for a sword and drew it out. Peter struck the servant of the high priest, cutting off his ear. "*Put your sword back in its place,*" Jesus said to him, "*for all who draw the sword will die by the sword*" (Matt 26:52; NIV). Then Jesus asked a question: **"Or do you think that I cannot now pray to my Father, and he will provide me with more than twelve legions of angels?"** (Matt 26:53). A legion was about six thousand soldiers, so Jesus was talking about seventy-two thousand angels that he could have called upon immediately. He was telling everyone present that the soldiers could not take him against his will. Jesus was in perfect alignment with the Father, exactly where he was supposed to be. God would have honored any wish from his Son. If Jesus had requested a legion of angels, he would have received them immediately! Jesus had complete control of the situation. God is a God of power and resources. When we do what he asks of us, we are tremendously energized and we will not falter or be weakened in any way. Jesus healed the man's ear, and they took Jesus away not because they had the power to do it but because Jesus allowed them to.

Jesus asked an unusual question, again not only to get religious leaders to ponder but also to provoke them. When Jesus's authority or alignment was challenged, he many times answered a question with a question. In the twenty-first chapter of Matthew, Jesus was again in the temple courts around the Colonnades, which was a great open area. The chief priests and elders came to Jesus and asked what authority allowed him to perform such incredible miracles, and who gave him this authority. What a question! When we are in alignment with our authorities and we are accomplishing things in a leadership capacity, at times we are asked the same question. Jesus had a reply for them. He said, **"I also will ask you one thing, which if you tell me, I likewise will tell you by what authority I do these things: The baptism of John—where was it from? From heaven or from men?"** (Matt 21:24–25; Mark 11:29-30; Luke 20:3–4).

Thousands of people were going to the wilderness by the Jordan River to see John the Baptist. He was baptizing them, and they were in awe! Many religious leaders were being baptized. They were turning toward the man that John said was coming after him, this Jesus whose sandals John claimed he was not fit to tie. Jesus asked the leaders and the chief priests where they felt John was receiving his authority of Baptism. Of course, had the priests replied that they believed John received his calling from heaven, Jesus would have challenged this belief and questioned their persecution of John. In fact, John was eventually killed! If the priests said that they believed John's gift was not of heaven, the people would have been upset, and the priests were afraid of the reaction from all the people who believed in John the Baptist. These people thought John the Baptist was a prophet; therefore, they were in trouble no matter how they answered. The Pharisees told Jesus that they did not know, and Jesus responded by refusing to tell them where his authority came from. He was not going to answer a question so trite. He was telling them what authority (alignment) he had by implication. Jesus let them know they had some issues to deal with concerning authority and alignment. When they dealt with those issues, he would talk to them about his authority.

We need to recognize the authority that we are under through total evaluation of all our resources. We need to question character, integrity, and effectiveness of ministry. We need to question reputation. We should not trust a person's reputation unless we get to know the person and have definite engagement with him or her or take time to make an objective evaluation. Gossip is part of human nature, now as well as in the time of Jesus. However, if we have integrity and are aligned with Jesus, we can be constantly challenged by it and never feel threatened. A sense of jealousy and indignation existed toward Jesus because he spoke with authority, as a man who was powerful, righteous, and had tremendous influence.

After Jesus was arrested, the high priests began to question him about his disciples and his teachings. They tried to trap him and to find something of which they could accuse him of. Jesus was telling them that he spoke openly to everybody all over the country. He was saying that he spoke in their temples and synagogues, and he never said anything in secret. Then Jesus asked them this question: **"Why do you ask Me?"** (John 18:21). He questioned why their questions were necessary. The priests could have asked one of the many people who heard Jesus speak. But the priests became so indignant that they struck Jesus right across the face. Then Jesus asked another question: **"If I have spoken evil, bear witness of the evil; but if well, why do you strike Me?"** (John 18:23).

There is something about a move of God that a bureaucracy or religious system has trouble handling. The major move today is toward the independent church. Many books have been written about how to build a large church. A completely different alignment of authority is being set up. At one time, the denominational church and high priests set the church alignment. There is now a great transfer of people out of denominational churches into independent churches, and there has been great resistance to this. A whole new movement of house churches may arise as it has in other countries. Would those who represent a legitimate move of God be struck across the face because they are proclaiming that they are in alignment with his precepts and what he is doing today? We must be very careful not to come against what Jesus is doing!

The Pharisees and the religious leaders were constantly questioning the authority of Jesus in the Scriptures. In Matthew 22, leaders came to Jesus, and attempting to placate him, stated, "Teacher we know you are a man of integrity, you teach in the way of God, you are not swayed by man, and you pay no attention to who they are" (Matt 22:16; NIV). Along with this compliment came a setup, as the leaders then asked: "Tell us therefore, what do you think? Is it lawful to pay taxes to Caesar, or not?" (Matt 22:17; NIV). Why, they wondered, should they be paying something to this earthly authority instead of to the church? It is a question of alignment. They tried to create a conflict so that no matter how Jesus replied, they could trip him up. So he asked them, **"Why do you test me, you hypocrites?"** (Matt 22:18; Mark 12:15; Luke 20:23). Then Jesus asked to look at a coin used to pay this tax. They brought a denarius to him, and he asked: **"Whose image and inscription is this?"** (Matt 22:20; Mark 12:16; Luke 20:24). They replied, "Caesar." He then told them: *"Render therefore to Caesar the things that are Caesar's, and to God the things that are God's"* (Matt 22:21; Mark 12:17; Luke 20:25).

When they heard this, they were amazed, and they left him. They just walked away. Jesus recognized their attempt to trap him. The religious leaders continually questioned Jesus's authority. These leaders were unable to realize that God had given Jesus his authority. God sets up all authority. There is alignment in government, in business, and in the church. God has alignment everywhere. We must respect that alignment and be careful to understand what it is all about. It is the blessing of life! All of the New Testament is full of alignments and loyalties toward authority.

John chapter 9 is solely dedicated to healing one man who had been blind since birth. In this particular scene, Jesus spit into the ground and made mud. He stuck this mud in the blind man's eyes and instructed him to wash in the pool of Siloam. So he went, and washed, and he was able to see. Eventually, the healed blind man went into the synagogue where he was chastised by the religious leaders who asked him who had healed him. They questioned whether this man was ever really blind in the first place. They found his parents to testify that he indeed was blind and could now see. Then they hurled insults at this man and actually threw him out of the temple!

When Jesus heard of this, he found the man he had healed. Jesus asked him a key question, the most important question of our lives today dealing with alignment and our position with the Lord. He asked him, **"Do you believe in the Son of God?"** (John 9:35). When the man replied affirmatively and questioned who he was, Jesus told him: *"You have both seen Him and it is He who is talking with you"* (John 9:37). The man then professed his belief in Jesus. Jesus told us, *"For judgment I have come into this world, that those who do not see may see, and those who see may be made blind"* (John 9:39). The question of the age is, do we believe in Jesus? If there is any confusion, Jesus makes it clear that he is the Son of God, the Great I Am, Lord of Lords. In other words, the boss!

In the very last section of John 21, Jesus indicated to Peter the type of death he could expect, one in which Peter would glorify God. Peter in turn replied by asking what would happen to John, the author of that particular gospel. Imagine the passion in the eyes of Jesus as he looked directly at Peter and replied, **"If I will that he remain till I come, what is that to you?"** (John 21:22–23). What a question! He was urging Peter not to concern himself with matters out of his control but instead focus on his own alignment with God. Jesus illustrated this by telling Peter to follow him. Why be concerned about judging others? Why be concerned about what others are saying and doing? That is God's business unless God directs us to intervene in a situation. What we need to seek is the alignment that Jesus has for us, just as he pointed out to Peter.

Another example of his authority and alignment occurred when Jesus asked something that would lead to one of the most powerful statements ever made anywhere in the Scriptures. Again, when the officials began to approach Jesus in preparation for his arrest, Jesus looked right at them and asked, **"Whom are you seeking?"** (John 18:4, 7). Knowing all, Jesus was setting them up for a revelation so powerful that they would be physically impacted by it. When they replied that they were looking for Jesus, he stated, *"I am he"* (John 18:5, 8). It was a declaration that literally floored the arresting officers. They all fell backwards to the ground. Nothing could have established a stronger authority to these men than those three words from Jesus. It was a reference to Yahweh in the Old Testament. He allowed himself to be revealed to these men as the true physical manifestation of God through his response, thus causing them to momentarily comprehend the magnificent power of his alignment with the Father in Heaven. Establishing and recognizing God's alignment is the most powerful resource we have.

The last question in this chapter occurred very early in Jesus's ministry. He met his first two disciples and they began to follow him. Jesus one day asked the two, **"What do you seek?"** (John 1:38). Jesus yet again asks a provocative, timeless question. If we consider Jesus to be the Son of God, the one we are to be aligned with, then he is asking us this very question. What do we want? What do we want from him? He is ready to give us an answer. All we need to do is ask him. When the disciples asked Jesus where he was staying, he told them to see for themselves. Of course, those disciples went with him and saw many things. Imagine following behind Jesus, having never met him, when suddenly he turns around, makes eye contact, and asks us what we want. He is asking us this today. Jesus wants us to follow him just as his disciples did. Jesus did everything his Father asked of him, a demonstration of perfect *spiritual alignment*. Jesus is urging us to strive for this same ideal. Jesus asks us to align ourselves wholeheartedly with him.

5

Spiritual Commitment

The Law of Agreement

THE DEFINITION

Commitment: A pledge or promise to do something. Dedication to a long-term course of action; engagement; involvement.

WEBSTER'S NEW WORLD DICTIONARY

COMMITMENT MAY be determined and defined by the level of dedication and participation. People who demonstrate a directed dedication usually have internal passion for their particular endeavors. An athlete trying out for a professional team is expected to be not only exceptionally talented but also wholeheartedly committed. It may take several seasons in the minors, multiple attempts in try-outs, and years of practice. During this initial process, the athlete will be focused mainly on the individual goal of making a team. Exerting a tremendous amount of effort for the benefit of all the other players and the fans should come later.

If this athlete's effort level is not maintained, if his commitment wanes, the coach will undoubtedly take notice. It will not be long before the coach talks to him about the effort he is applying relative to his capabilities. The conversation, while acknowledging the player's talents, will inevitably address the need for increased and sustained commitment and dedication to ensure success. It might be noted that others have also noticed the player's waning level of commitment. Failure on the part of the player to respond accordingly would ultimately result in his or her removal from the team. Scenarios of this sort occur frequently in sports, business, and in other types of relationships.

THE BRIDGE

Jesus addressed the commitment level of people by comparing life issues to the Kingdom of God. The principles presented through his interrogation of people apply to every part of life. When it comes to commitment and involvement concerning the Kingdom, Jesus revealed that there is no room for ambivalence. Total dedication and commitment to the values of his Kingdom are of utmost importance to Jesus.

Success in any endeavor cannot be achieved through lackadaisical effort. A passionate and sustained determination is necessary. This is the prerequisite to enroll and participate in the realm called the Kingdom of Heaven. The level of commitment is relative to the success of an agreement to be part of this Kingdom.

Deciding to enter into and be a part of the spiritual life is the act one takes when making an empirical decision. It will change one's entire life. A person's life is entirely changed upon joining the armed forces. He or she will enter basic training, wear a uniform, fall in line, and learn different marches and formations. Everything will be done in coordination with everybody else, with the intention of eliminating personal agendas for the sake of the whole. When the armed forces accomplish the task of gaining a soldier's identity, it is personified by the soldier losing his or her ability and will to follow his or her own rules.

In the armed services, service people have little opportunity to choose their itineraries from day to day. Not much leeway exists for schedule changes. If a serviceperson disobeys commands, he or she receives disciplinary action that can sometimes lead to a court-martial. If a serious enough offense occurs, a dishonorable discharge or prison might result. But discipline in the armed services is acutely structured to thwart peer pressure. Exhibiting signs of rebellion thus results in serious consequences to the violator.

The principles of submission and authority apply to many areas of life. For many, it is not easy to submit. We may like to do as we please, but there are rules to every engagement. In this manner, Jesus applied regulations, models, and laws of commitment. Leaders tend to focus more on the commitment level of an individual than on their abilities. Jesus was no different in his approach. He made comments such as, "*Whoever finds his life will lose it, and whoever loses his life for my sake will find it*" (Matt 10:39; NIV). He was implying that life in the Kingdom is defined by our commitment to Kingdom principles, not based on its benefits. Life presents us with a variety of commitment affirmations. One of them is marriage, a matter of commitment and covenant. Our commitment level will be recognized by our value of the covenant.

When we speak of personal obligations, we are defining the elements that make up a commitment. A contract will always have conditions, clauses, contingencies, and considerations. Arbitrators and attorneys utilize them to prevent the misuse of power or misappropriation of terms. The terms of a contract are based upon the value of its commitment. If the conditions are not secure, the contract is not applicable. All of the contingencies must be met in order to meet the requirements for closure.

THE QUESTIONS

An example or use of the indemnity of words that make up a compulsory agreement is called a "covenant." Jesus demonstrated this by using the term "salt." Jesus leveraged his approach when addressing the lack of integrity in commitment when he presented this idea. He said to his followers, **"You are the salt of the earth. But if the salt looses its flavor, how shall it be seasoned?"** (Matt 5:13; Mark 9:50; Luke 14:34.) Salt is an item that brings flavor. It enhances vegetables or meats. But if it loses its saltiness, it is reduced to no effect and it loses its value. The efficiency of an ingredient determines its value or function. In this case, Jesus was using salt as a comparison and relating it as a practical application for commitment to the Kingdom of God.

In the Church, there are various degrees of commitment. There are leaders who are part of the force that effects change. There are also attendees, who congregate with varying levels of commitment but are obligated to do little else other than show up, listen, and leave. Some participate in certain projects and remain uninvolved in others, perpetuating the notion that just doing one little part is sufficient for the enhancement of the Church and God's Kingdom. Jesus directly addresses this notion of partial commitment through his question regarding salt. He is urging us to be leaders, to commit ourselves to be passionate and thoroughly involved in the causes of the Kingdom.

The pledge of a leader is demonstrated through total effort to create positive results. Regardless of position, the method of commitment is verified through achievement. Addressing the crowds with his salt analogy, Jesus illustrates the possibility and potential to lose effectiveness. Which is worse, being an involved, influential leader who is dedicated entirely to a cause, only to lose interest and eventually give up on the very principles that ensured success, or maintaining a peripheral position and never impacting anyone or anything? Both, Jesus assured, have consequences.

Two disciples came to Jesus and asked, "When you establish your kingdom, can we sit on your right or left?" He solemnly answered, **"Are you able to drink the cup that I am about to drink, and be baptized with the baptism that I am baptized with?"** (Matt 20:22; Mark 10:38). Comprehension of this statement requires understanding the meaning behind the word "cup." Jesus of Nazareth was about to undergo incredible suffering, the ultimate sacrifice for the sins of the world. This sacrifice would be the greatest demonstration of love recorded in history, and it developed the inauguration of the Kingdom on earth through the church. In answering the two disciples, Jesus used the word "cup" as a metaphor to represent the suffering he would soon endure. He was insinuating that these two disciples really had no idea of the persecution involved in following in Jesus's footsteps and was asking them if they were willing to completely sacrifice their lives for him and for his Kingdom.

These two, like the rest of the disciples, were novice in their understanding of the sacrifice required to be an integral part of God's Kingdom. They were getting a lesson in Kingdom commitment. We should question our commitment level just as Jesus questioned that of his disciples. Do we have the faith and spiritual strength to withstand our current crisis? Are we willing to do whatever is necessary to reach the other side? Are we looking for shortcuts, or do we possess the commitment needed to achieve our goals? Jesus questioned if the disciples had any inkling of the persecution he was soon to endure and questioned their willingness to stand firm in the face of such persecution in order to sit by his side in heaven.

In relationships, the level of involvement and commitment to the relationship will determine its success. When a stranger becomes an acquaintance, there is a small change in the commitment level. However, when this stranger becomes a friend and eventually a spiritual sibling, the commitment level deepens, leading to a more intense relationship. Committing oneself entirely to a relationship is a life-altering decision, and Jesus was asking if we are willing to make the decision to fully commit to him.

Jesus asked another question relating to commitment when he was teaching at the temple. He asked, **"Did not Moses give you the law, yet none of you keeps the law? Why do you seek to kill Me?"** (John 7:19). He was geared up to dispute hypocrisy and did so by reminding the religious leaders that they were not altogether diligent in their adherence to the Law of Moses. He was pointing out, as he did many times, the hypocrisy of the religious system. Jesus was troubled by how they exercised their authority. First, they did not fulfill the real purpose of the Law—to love, nurture, and provide a spiritually protective covering and a fatherly supervision. Also, time and again the religious leaders used their power and their position to benefit themselves without concern for the people. Jesus shed light on their abuses of power by questioning their true commitment to the laws of Moses and in doing so, exposed the hypocrisy prevalent in their hearts.

What are the standards for leadership? Is it possible that once people reach a higher status at work, in politics, or in a social society that they have gained the right to enforce rules that are no longer applicable to themselves? What is right? Should people of professional or exalted status receive special attention in legal, political, or social arenas? If not, who sets the standard? Who then can correct the system if the system is corrupt?

On a similar occasion, Jesus asked another question, **"Is a lamp brought to be put under a basket or under a bed? Is it not to be set on a lampstand?"** (Mark 4:21). Jesus was telling his followers that if they were going to commit themselves to the Kingdom of God, their actions should demonstrate that commitment. The level of commitment to an endeavor is determined by one's actions toward achieving that endeavor. Their dedication to the process involved in achieving their goal will reveal their level of commitment. This is true in all facets of life. For instance, the athlete discussed earlier this chapter can demonstrate commitment by practicing passionately and exerting a diligent effort. There is an electrifying aspect to those who have a strong, dedicated commitment. It is contagious, and it motivates others to action. A light shines through us when we are excited about what we are doing. People will notice the impact that we make when we are fully committed. It reflects all around us, and we see it in any activity, job, or relationship. Jesus tells us that our light will shine if our commitment is strong.

Some Greeks came to see Jesus, and he was giving a discourse, saying that we must lay down our lives like a seed in the ground and then we will bear fruit. He then mentioned that his soul was troubled concerning his inevitable suffering. So he asked, "**. . . And what shall I say, Father save Me from this hour?**" (John 12:27). Then he answered his own question by stating that his suffering was his purpose. His commitment was to lay down his life.

Before Jesus was arrested, he went into a garden to pray. He asked his closest disciples, Peter, James, and John, to wait nearby and keep watch while praying with him. While praying alone, he cried out to the Father, "*My Father, if it is possible, may this cup be taken from me*" (Matt 26:39; NIV). This passage of Scripture has often been misunderstood. Let us look again at the word "cup." Besides its literal meaning, symbolically it is used as a metaphor representing life itself, an expression of destiny in both the good and evil sense. But the primary use by the prophets is the cup of sorrow. It symbolizes the cup of God's punishment, vengeance, and judgment (Isa 51:17, 22; Lam 4:21; Ps 11:6, 75:8). The wine cup is a representation of God's passionate wrath (Rev 14:8, 10; 16:19; 18:3; 19:15).

When Jesus referred to the cup, he was referring to the judgment of God, which was placed upon him. He became God's suffering servant, our substitute for sin. He received the initial judgment of God while praying. The physical manifestation was sweat as drops of blood. The weight of this burden was so overwhelming that Jesus was exhausted to the point of death. The heaviness of this assault weakened him. He was experiencing tremendous emotional and physical trauma. But was this God's plan? Was this where Jesus said he would die? No, it is clear that he understood his plight would take the form of a Roman cross. The goal and purpose of becoming a human was his death and resurrection, and without the shedding of his blood, there could be no forgiveness of sin (Heb 9:22).

While praying in the Garden of Gethsemane, his sweat was like drops of blood falling to the ground (Luke 22:44). His physical condition was rapidly weakening. However, Jesus was willing to do whatever the Father willed. Thus he said, *"Nevertheless, not my will but thine be done"* (Luke 22:42; KJV). The answer was given when an angel came and strengthened Jesus. He was not to die there but to go to the cross. His prayer was answered, and God gave him the ability to continue with the plan of redemption. This is one of the most remarkable illustrations of commitment. Jesus was committed to fulfilling God's plan regardless of the possible adjustments. He was not rethinking his decision, wanting to find a way out. He was rather trying to follow the Father regardless of the cost.

During this trauma, he went back to where his friends were sleeping. He asked, **"What! Could you not watch with me one hour?"** (Matt 26:40; Mark 14:37). Jesus was chiding them for their lack of commitment to him during this intensely dark period. When he returned again, he found them in the same position, and again asked, **"Are you still sleeping and resting?"** (Matt 26:45; Mark 14:41; Luke 22:46). Again, Jesus was disappointed at the absence of commitment evident in those who were supposed to be his closest and most dedicated followers.

On another occasion, Jesus turned to Peter and asked him, **"Will you lay down your life for my sake?"** (John 13:38). Jesus knew that Peter, a fisherman by trade, had family and other obligations. Jesus was asking if Peter was willing to let it all go to follow him. Jesus was not asking Peter to violate one Kingdom commitment for the sake of another. He was, however, questioning the willingness of Peter to rearrange his priorities in order to align himself completely with Jesus and his will.

Are we willing to live a different life? Are we willing to act differently, to commit ourselves entirely to Jesus, and to make this commitment part of the very essence of what we do from now on? The whole issue of commitment is to understand the real depth of the question. Jesus is asking if we understand the requirements of Kingdom life. They are life-changing requirements. People make commitments to one another in various levels of relationship, and whatever level that might be, it is important to understand the level of commitment or expectation that we are agreeing to. Jesus questioned Peter about laying down his life because that is what commitment to the Kingdom is all about. It is not something to be stepped into halfway.

The Bible refers to us as fellowshipping with his sufferings or being crucified with him. This is not an issue to be taken lightly, as there is no middle ground. In the Church today, most leaders would agree that the main issue is the level of dedication of people. These leaders would like to see Christians really take hold of the Kingdom. Maybe we should follow the example set by Jesus over two thousand years ago and redefine what commitment to the Kingdom really means. We hesitate to define this commitment, because in doing so, we risk losing those who are content to sit on the fence and remain only somewhat or not at all committed. In some cases it will affect the finances of churches and projects with which they are involved.

A major concern in the church today is people leaving. Attendance in church fluctuates in competition with various outside activities. The movie *The Passion* was released and church attendance rose as a result. The tragedy of 9/11 also caused a temporarily dramatic increase in church attendance. However, we must ask ourselves, was this momentum maintained, and did it effect positive change in the Kingdom? If so, how long is it going to last? How long will the effectiveness be felt? Is it affecting our culture? Is the light of Jesus continually shining brightly through us? Jesus is asking those of us in the Kingdom, both leaders and followers, how strong our commitment is to him. Is it a life-changing experience? Do we recognize that our lives are going to be totally altered? The leadership of Christ is an important dimension that involves all aspects of life. Jesus was willing to address it. He was willing to face the consequences of his *spiritual commitment* regardless of how people responded. Are we?

6

Spiritual Provisions

Defining the Realm of Benefits

THE DEFINITION

Provision: Something provided, prepared, or supplied for the future; a preparatory arrangement or measure taken in advance for meeting some future need.

WEBSTER'S NEW WORLD DICTIONARY

PROVISION MAY be received in the immediate future or in the long term. Regardless of its timeframe, the emphasis is that it is available to us. For some, provision takes the form of tangible assets such as bank accounts, securities, bonds, and retirement funds. However, in a properly understood spiritual sense, it is the guarantee of security without the need for substance. It is based on faith and is inherently difficult for us to trust. Considering all the disappointments we face in everyday life such as betrayal, rejection, the absence of integrity, failed relationships, and so on, how can we trust anything or anybody? This applies especially in the realm of spiritual benefits or provisions. Who will supply them? Will they come through? Will they be there when I need them? How can I trust a God I cannot see?

THE BRIDGE

When Jesus spoke about provision, he was implicating that those who are in the Kingdom of God can have assurance that provision is available. Those new to or not part of the Kingdom may have difficulty understanding how provision can be guaranteed without it first being obtained. When speaking of his provision, Jesus thus repeatedly asked his audience, "Do you not understand?" He wanted us to be assured that our reliance and trust in God is what brings about this provision. Without our trust in him, provision is not available. Jesus admonishes us to trust him for provision for our spiritual life.

Some do not have the faith that God will supply all of our needs according to his riches in glory. Usually the doubt is a result of hardships, broken promises, or difficult times that have not warranted any hope. Our confidence level diminishes when we look at our circumstances as they are currently, instead of what they can be. One evening, when a storm approached while the disciples were in a boat with Jesus, they became very frightened. Jesus was sleeping, and their fears overpowered them. Despite the miracles they had witnessed Jesus perform, the storm reassured them only of their imminent demise.

THE QUESTIONS

Why would the disciples be so concerned? Is it any different today? Most of us feel like we are in a boat, and even if we know the Lord, the seas are rough, and fear and anxiety can overtake us. We have heard so many reassuring testimonies of people in similar circumstances who have trusted in and prayed to God for deliverance. Yet these disciples had spent months with Jesus and they could not predict what he would do. So when he asked, **"Why are you fearful, O you of little faith?"** (Matt 8:26; Mark 4:40; Luke 8:25), they probably were taken aback as we would be today.

Many of us are fearful. Fear is a very powerful force that causes us to make decisions and come to conclusions that reveal our faith. How we react to anxiety will directly affect our life. In many ways, the force of fear questions and undermines our trust. In the New Testament, Paul stated that fear and intimidation are not of the Lord but rather love and a sound mind (2 Tim 1:7). Fear defines our reliance and reveals to us on whom we depend.

On another occasion when the disciples were out to sea, Jesus repeated this saying, **"O you of little faith, why did you doubt?"** (Matt 14:31). Jesus walked out on the water and beckoned for Peter to join him. Peter stepped out of the boat and started walking toward him, but then he became fearful and began to sink. Jesus then saved him. Calling for Peter to join him on the water was akin to Jesus directly promising to care for and protect Peter.

During another instance, Jesus used even stronger words: **"O faithless and perverse generation, how long shall I be with you? How long shall I bear with you?"** (Matt 17:17; Mark 9:19). This question came about as a man brought his son who was having seizures, suffering, and falling into fire to Jesus for healing. The disciples could not heal this boy, and Jesus was deeply disappointed, because they did not believe that they could. These disciples lacked the intensity, engagement, and trust in God to receive the provision necessary to heal the child.

When Jesus repeated the phrase, "O you of little faith," he was demonstrating his frustration in the lack of trust from those who supposedly knew him best. Why is it that we do not believe that he can do extraordinary things? There is an innate block in our way of thinking in our nature, that gets in the way of our absolute trust in him. He is the One who created this universe and maintains life's processes. Is there a sense that we do not always trust God? Do we trust him for our marriages, our business, or in our spiritual life?

Jesus made it clear, as mentioned in other chapters, that he called leaders of churches to empower and train others to be involved. Everyone is intended to be a minister. Everybody has the power to do something positive. This is why spiritual offices are given to build up the Church (Eph 4:7–16).

Early in Jesus's ministry, he addressed a crowd with several famous exhortations, now referred to as the Sermon on the Mount. He asked this question: **"Now if God so clothes the grass of the field, which today is, and tomorrow is thrown into the oven, will He not much more clothe you, O you of little faith?"** (Matt 6:30; Luke 12:28). This was a strong statement to the listeners. He was pointing out that if God can grow the wheat that we put into an oven, is that not a sign that he is the source of the wheat? If he provides the sun's ray and the chemical process to enable the process of creation, then why would he not take care of us, his ultimate creation?

The discipleship approach that Jesus promoted and patterned is to be our prototype. He poured his life into these twelve men and into the assembly of believers who followed him for over three years. One time Jesus went into a building where there were two men, both blind and calling out for him to heal them. Jesus asked them: **"Do you believe that I am able to do this?"** (Matt 9:28). He had healed other blind men, and they were sure he could heal them also. He touched their eyes and healed them because they had faith that he could. Jesus provided proportionally according to their declaration of faith. There is a certain level of trust, belief, and reliance on the Lord that God honors. These men believed, and they were healed. We can ask God to give us more faith and he will.

At another time, there were again two blind men, this time along the side of the road. These two men were also begging Jesus for mercy, hoping to be healed. The crowd rebuked them to discontinue their pleading. But the two kept shouting louder and louder. They really wanted Jesus to come over and see them. And so Jesus stopped and asked a very strange question: **"What do you want me to do for you?"** (Matt 20:32; Mark 10:51; Luke 18:41). This is not the only time Jesus asked this question to blind men.

Why would Jesus even ask this question? Somehow, Jesus was able to get people to go inside themselves, to introspect and evaluate, to look at things from a new perspective. It is the nature of God to ask us what we want. The two blind men simply replied that they wanted their sight restored. Jesus, of course, had compassion and immediately healed them, and they became followers. However, he first wanted to hear them verbalize their desire for his divine healing, and in doing so, they pleased him by demonstrating their faith in his miraculous power.

Today Jesus is asking us all what he can do for us. What are the desires of our heart? What is it that we need from him? He will always be there for us, providing we reach out and search for him with all of our strength. By using the interrogative, Jesus forced people to reveal what they were anticipating from their situation. He loves to provide for those who call out in desperation to him. The numerous interrogatives used by Jesus reveal his empirical approach. He is trying to tell us something.

There was a man lying near a pool, which was called Bethesda. This pool was rumored to have healing powers. Legend held that the first person to enter it when the water churned would be instantly healed. A man who was paralyzed had been lying there for thirty-eight years. Jesus approached him and asked: **"Do you want to be made well?"** (John 5:6). This man had been waiting decades for healing, and yet Jesus asked this most obvious question, as if he didn't know the answer.

Does the Church want to do the things that God has called it to do and have an impact on the culture and the people around it? Through his disciple John, Jesus expressed this concern when he wrote seven letters to seven churches (Rev 2–3). While on the island of Patmos, John penned letters that could very well have been written to a contemporary crowd today. Is it possible that although today's churches have a lot of good things going on, they have lost their first love? That's what Jesus wrote to the Church in Ephesus. Are some churches lukewarm and in jeopardy of being spit out like the Church in Laodicea (Rev 3:16)? Is their reputation of "being alive," as he spoke about the Church in Sardis (Rev 3:1), exaggerated?

The paralytic man waiting for decades by the pool was obviously handicapped. Yet still Jesus asked him what he wanted. The cripple replied that he had nobody to help him into the pool, and when he would attempt to struggle into the water, someone would always cast him aside. Upon hearing this, Jesus commanded the man to pick up his bed and walk. Even in the face of impossibility, the faith of the believer brings possibility. For this man provision was not a hot meal, it was a restored life. Can this happen with a repentant Church?

Jesus brought provision in an astounding way to four thousand people through a miraculous feeding. They had been following Jesus and his posse for some distance and time. Everybody was hungry, and the disciples discussed amongst themselves their dilemma of having no food. They believed that there was no way humanly possible to feed the throng. So Jesus asked his close followers this question: **"How many loaves do you have?"** (Matt 15:34; Mark 8:5). Jesus, of course, knew that there was no way to physically obtain the amount of bread needed, and with thousands of hungry followers, the actual answer of seven loaves clearly made the question moot. So why would Jesus ask this question? He asked it because he wanted his disciples to ponder their plight for a moment. What did they have without Jesus? How could this situation, where people needed immediate sustenance, be handled? Who was going to take leadership? Jesus then took charge, made the crowd sit down, and began breaking bread, which kept multiplying, and of course, everyone was fed. Provision was needed, and Jesus provided abundantly.

In the gospels, as previously mentioned in chapter two, "Spiritual Life," Jesus discussed with the disciples the yeast of the Pharisees. The disciples were confused by this discussion and worried because they had not brought their leftover bread. Knowing their concerns, Jesus again asked: **"Do you not yet understand, or remember the five loaves of the five thousand and how many baskets you took up?"** (Matt 16:9; Mark 8:17). Why would Jesus be talking about provision or the need for food? Why were the disciples worried about it? Jesus was reminding them that he could provide for any need at any time and that he was there for those who ask for and have faith in his provision.

In the last stage of Jesus's ministry, one of his final conversations with the disciples was when Jesus prophesied to Peter that he would deny him. Peter was convinced that he was ready to die with or for Jesus. It was in this setting that Jesus asked Peter this question: **"When I sent you without money bag, knapsack, and sandals, did you lack anything?"** (Luke 22:35). He was talking about the time he sent the disciples out to the cities to spread the Kingdom of God (Luke 9:1). Peter and the disciples affirmed that Jesus did provide for them. It was customary that people going on a trip were to have some food for their provisions. But in this case, Jesus was saying to them that it would be provided for them as a sign that they were part of the Kingdom. His point was that although temptation and hardship undoubtedly lie ahead for them during their journey, he would invariably be the solution to any difficulty they might encounter. If they called on Jesus and trusted in him, he would be there with an answer. All they had to do was have faith that he would choose the proper path for them.

He is still asking the same question to those who are currently attempting to spread the Kingdom of God. Does he not make apparent the fact that provision is always available to us? Doesn't he clearly show us where we need to be and what he is doing in our lives? Has he not provided answers to our prayers?

Maybe these answers were not exactly what we wanted to hear, or maybe they were not provided in a timeline that suits us, but he was most definitely listening and he provided the answers we needed when we needed them. He is the one who knows what is best for us. Are we aware of that?

Jesus told a story where a man had sowed seed into his field. While he was sleeping one night, his enemy came along and sowed tares (bad seed) into the field. When the wheat sprouted up, it formed heads and so did the weeds. His servants ran to the farmer and asked: "... **'Sir, did you not sow good seed in your field?'**" (Matt 13:27). Jesus is really asking this question through the servants' query to the farmer. Where did the weeds come from? Even when we are involved in expanding the Kingdom, and the Church is doing its job and individuals are out sowing their seed, planting, watering, and really accomplishing something, there are still going to be weeds. Something will always attack our provision!

The question thus remains, where do the weeds come from? The answer is that they come from the enemy of all that is good and productive. Jesus is telling us that Satan is responsible for the weeds of destruction and death, and they are part of the battle in which we are involved. The more active we are, the more fields we plow, and the more seeds we sow, the more these weeds will creep in and the more things will come against us. The servants in this story asked the landowner if they should pull up the destructive weeds, which would serve as a metaphor for destroying the enemies of the Lord.

Do we attack those who are causing us problems? No, because pulling up the weeds would result in some of the good seed being uprooted also. So the story goes that the landowner instructed the servants to let both the weeds and the good product grow until harvest, at which time the weeds were to be gathered and separated from the wheat, which would still be healthy. The weeds, representing evil, would expose themselves to such a degree and come to such apostasy that they wouldn't harm nor be confused with the good product. Jesus will provide protection! That is the reason he told this parable. Let us be careful that we do not try to take on something that God has not given us protection to do. He is the one who strengthens us. He told us to turn the other cheek and to love and forgive our brother. The Lord said that vengeance would be his. He will provide the proper solution to the problem if we just wait on and trust him.

On three different occasions (Matt 6:30; 8:26; 14:31), Jesus used the same phrase in his questions. As he asked the question, he planted this phrase in the context of some of the questions: "*O you of little faith*." In a similar fashion, Jesus told us not to be afraid of those who can hurt our bodies but have no effect on our souls. He continued by asking: **"Are not two sparrows sold for a copper coin?"** (Matt 10:29; Luke 12:6). During the time of Jesus, sparrows were not of much worth monetarily. They were very common and of little economic value. Yet sparrows could be seen everywhere. Because of the abundance of sparrows, little attention was given to them. Despite this, he said: "*And not one of them falls to the ground apart from your Father's will. But the very hairs of your head are all numbered. Do not fear therefore; you are of more value than many sparrows*" (Matt 10:29–31). God provides for the sparrows. Being that we as humans are much more important than a bird, doesn't it make sense that he will most certainly provide for us?

God has a divine plan, a purpose, and a destiny for every person's life. To expand God's Kingdom, we do not need to depend upon anything but him. Is it possible that many have never achieved confidence in God for his provisions because of lost hopes based upon irrational declarations by today's television preachers? Have seed faith promises bankrupted families and brought mistrust in the body of Christ? Do gimmicks, bargains, marketing schemes, and flashy guarantees make us trade our faith for a methodology? Is there a get-rich scheme invading the

Church? What would Jesus say if he was on Christian television today? Would he guarantee Cadillacs, or would he provide hope for our broken dreams, bodies, and destinies? There is a *spiritual provision* that can calm every storm. There is a blessing that comes from God that will meet every need. Our future depends on it, and we today can receive it. Jesus said so!

7

Spiritual Revelations

Communication through Disclosures and Discovery

THE DEFINITION

Revelation: A revealing, or disclosing of something; something disclosed; disclosure, especially a striking disclosure, as of something not previously known or realized; God's disclosure or manifestation to humanity of himself and his will.

Webster's New World Dictionary

Revelation is a divine disclosure. God has inscribed his revelation to us in a book. "All Scripture is given by inspiration of God . . ." (2 Tim 3:16). This revelation did not come "by the will of man . . ." but as holy prophets of old were ". . . moved by the Holy Spirit" (2 Pet 1:21). The Bible is God's inspired and complete objective revelation to us (2 Tim 3:16–17).

We can have revelations from God for our special use when he knows we need it, but God's revelation is a lifelong and continual work of his spirit within us.

THE BRIDGE

God speaks to our hearts through his word by his Spirit. The Spirit of God never leads contrary to the word of God. God desires to reach our hearts, but he does not bypass our heads on the way to our hearts. "*Come now, let us reason together, says the Lord*" (Isa 1:18). Paul said, "Whatever is true ... think about such things" (Phil 4:8; NIV). And Peter added, "... Give the reason for the hope that you have" (1 Pet 3:15; NIV). Nonetheless, God does want to open our hearts by his Spirit to the truth he has revealed in his word.

THE QUESTIONS

God reveals what Jesus brings us to by asking certain questions for which only he can provide answers. The concepts embodied in his questions were not common among people of his day and would not be common now if we did not have knowledge of his word. Jesus once asked Peter, James, and John: **"And how is it written concerning the Son of Man, that he must suffer many things and be treated with contempt?"** (Mark 9:12). The nation of Israel and the Jews were seeking the Messiah whom they believed would come as a king, assume complete control of their land and communities, and in the process, free them from Roman oppression. This king would have the authority and position to protect them for the remainder of their lives. They were not looking for a Savior, even though Jesus made reference to the Old Testament Scriptures a number of times. In doing so, he showed them how the Scriptures indeed did indicate that they needed a Savior, a sacrificial lamb that would die an extraordinary death, and who would be the atonement for all people who believe in him.

However, before Jesus asked this above question, he was asked why the teachers of the law insisted that Elijah must come before the Messiah. Jesus indicated that indeed, Elijah did come first. He told them how Elijah existed in the form of John the Baptist, whom they killed, just as the Scriptures predicted. Then Jesus asked this question regarding the suffering of the Son of Man. Neither Peter nor James nor John knew how to answer this question. It was a revealing type of question designed to get them to understand that he was the Lamb that was prophesied about in the book of Isaiah and in other places in the Scripture. He was to come and lay down his life as atonement, a sacrifice of his blood for the forgiveness of sins. This was a concept beyond comprehension for most of them at this time, and many never could put aside their engrained notions long enough to recognize his truth.

Jesus emphasized this point in another question he asked while speaking to the Jews who were persecuting him for breaking the Sabbath and for claiming to be the Son of God. He first stated that he would not accuse them before God, that Moses, in whom they had placed all of their hope, would instead accuse them. Jesus then told them that if they truly believed Moses, they would believe him, because Jesus was the one whom Moses wrote about. Jesus again was trying to reveal himself to them. He then asked this question: **"But if you do not believe his writings, how will you believe my words?"** (John 5:47). The Jewish leaders did not interpret the Old Testament Scriptures properly. If they had, the true identity of Jesus would have been revealed to them. They exalted Moses as a great leader and prophet but did not listen closely to what he said, and thus would also not listen to or believe Jesus. This is a key question to all of us: Do we really believe in what Jesus says? Do we truly believe in him and in why he came?

In chapter three, "Spiritual Relationships," we refer to a revelatory dialogue that Jesus had with the people around him. He was telling a crowd that his flesh is food indeed, and those who eat Jesus's flesh and drink his blood abide in him and he in them. He was talking about partaking of himself, coming into true communion, becoming intimate and close, and absorbing him entirely (John 6:53–60). As he shared these things, he asked a question: **"Does this offend you?"** (John 6:61). He knew that what he spoke about indeed offended them, so much so that many of his disciples turned away from him. This was an entirely new concept, one that, at first, the Jews interpreted literally. But Jesus was really attempting to bring to their understanding the necessity of having a deep, intimate relationship with him. The Church needs to hear this again today. It may offend us, but we may need to hear it now more than ever. Jesus intended us to not only have an intimate relationship with him but also with each other.

Two pastors had churches directly across the street from each other. They rarely spoke to one another, and their congregations never had fellowship or communion together. One pastor eventually went through a very difficult time, and his people turned against him because he was trying to move them forward and change their hearts just as Jesus was doing two thousand years ago. Opposition arose and they eventually asked him to leave. He became a chaplain at a military base in southern California, but just before he left, he came to a pastors' retreat at a camp called Dunklin, west of Stuart, Florida. At this retreat, the pastors separated into groups. They came from different cities, up and down the coast of Florida, and this particular pastor happened to end up in the group with the pastor who had the church across the street from his. He began to share that he was leaving soon and told his story to the pastors in his group.

After the session was over, his counterpart from across the street got up and expressed his disbelief that this fellow pastor, directly across the street, had suffered and hurt greatly and was in dire straits in regard to his family and his leadership. The most disheartening thing was that these two pastors, existing for so long in such close proximity to one another, had never forged any type of relationship! They never related to each other even though they were right across the street. The second pastor wept as he spoke, asking the troubled pastor to forgive him in front of the others. Many other pastors, at least sixty or seventy were there. It was a very sad time. Nevertheless, it is all too typical of where we are today. If Jesus reveals the true meaning of drinking his blood and eating his flesh, of truly partaking of him, will we be offended? It needs not to be a symbol, but rather something of the heart. The Lord wants us to be much closer in communion with him and with each other than we really are.

Jesus once conversed with Nicodemus, a leader of the Pharisees who was part of the Jewish council. Jesus was explaining the Kingdom of God to Nicodemus, telling him how we must be born again. When Nicodemus expressed his confusion regarding the concept of spiritual rebirth, Jesus compared people born of the Holy Spirit to the wind, in that it goes where it pleases, and although it can be heard, the direction is difficult to determine. Jesus was talking about the Holy Spirit, about accepting him and his word, and ultimately about being reborn into God's Kingdom. Of course, these concepts were beyond comprehension for the literal-minded Nicodemus. He just couldn't understand Jesus's message. It was an incredible revelation to him, as to all people through the ages. Jesus then asked: **"Are you the teacher of Israel, and do not know these things?"** (John 3:10).

He was dismayed that Nicodemus, a member of the Jewish ruling council who was responsible for teaching God's chosen people, was clueless about Jesus and his power of atonement. How many leaders do we have today who are teaching our people and are ignorant like Nicodemus? Jesus is asking this question right now to our entire society. How many teachers are there who do not know or do not understand the importance of accepting Christ, coming into the Kingdom, and being born again? This episode was a great indictment on the leader Nicodemus. He was teaching all of these people in Israel, supposedly on God's behalf, and yet he was not teaching them the most important message of all, that of God's deliverance of humanity from sin through the sacrifice of His Son Jesus!

One of the most significant questions that Jesus asked was again directed at Nicodemus: **"If I have told you earthly things and you do not believe, how will you believe if I tell you heavenly things?"** (John 3:12). Jesus talked about practical issues and revealed himself not only through miracles, but also through parables and stories that related to everyday life. When Jesus told Nicodemus that whoever believes in him would have eternal life, he was asking Nicodemus and the people of his time, as well as ours, to really internalize and understand that it is the greatest revelation ever bestowed upon us. The revelation from God, the person of Jesus and his character, and the very essence of his being is an extraordinary phenomenon. It is the answer to all of the spiritual yearnings and doubts of mankind, although many of us cannot or do not want to recognize it.

Phillip, one of the disciples, had that problem. He asked Jesus to show the disciples his Father and they would be satisfied. They had seen firsthand many of his miracles, so Jesus answered this request by asking a question: **"Do you not believe that I am in the Father, and the Father in me?"** (John 14:10). The disciples couldn't fathom the idea that Jesus was God's revelation to mankind, that he was the manifestation of God in human flesh. Jesus had done things no man ever could in the miracles that he performed and yet they still desired more proof. This also seems to be true of many Christians today. How many times we have cried out to the Lord, pleading for his help? He comes through time and again, and yet we still lack faith that the Father is always with us. Jesus is saying this very thing to us today. We have read his word, we have knowledge of his incredible works, and we have witnessed his love and work in our lives, yet we still want more. Doubt and fear, as it was with Phillip, may be as prominent today in us, and even in the Church, than it was when Jesus revealed himself as a human being two thousand years ago.

In chapter 2, we referred to a passage from Mark 8. Jesus was talking to the disciples about the yeast of the Pharisees and that of Herod. He was explaining how bureaucracies and hierarchies could burden systems of human service, both secular and religious, and eventually begin to oppress the very people they were created to serve. He was warning them about the oppressive nature of bureaucracy. He mentioned yeast, causing the disciples to believe that it was because they forgot the bread that was broken when Jesus fed his followers. They hadn't brought the bread with them and the abundance left over, so they thought Jesus was talking about that. With their flawed logic in mind, Jesus asked them some revealing questions: **"Why do you reason because you have no bread? Do you not yet perceive nor understand? Is your heart still hardened? Having eyes, do you not see? And having ears, do you not hear? And do you not remember?"** (Mark 8:17–18). Jesus was prompting them to stretch their comprehension beyond the physical, to understand that he was actually discussing concepts of the spiritual realm. He was warning them of what can happen when we adhere to man-made systems and in doing so, is warning us about what is happening today.

We come into his spiritual Kingdom full of fresh life. We love the Lord. We develop a deeper sense of spiritual awareness and want to mature in our spirituality. Then suddenly we encounter some insidious form of the yeast of the Pharisees that Jesus warned us about. The disciples couldn't see it, and we don't seem to be able to see it today. Man has a tendency to structure things to such a degree that the spirit of an endeavor becomes muted because of bureaucratic stagnancy, which becomes institutionalized and thus corrupts many organizations and structures. Our government in America has become so big that we must have tax increases or endure deficits before efforts to curtail growth of bureaucracies are taken. Once a deficit has gotten out of control, there cannot be more people added to the government, and eventually it must be reduced in size, but the dependence on government has been engrained into our systems. Bureaucracy robs religious and governmental systems of the ability to flow with the needs and requirements of the moment.

It is like having a personal budget. Sometimes there are good times and we flourish. We can spend more. Then there are times the income is not as great, and we have to restrict spending. If we don't flow and adjust to those times, our lives can become unbalanced. When Jesus warned about the yeast of the Pharisees, he was compelling us to flow with the direction of the Spirit. Jesus was warning us to watch out for this yeast. It can come upon us and restrict revelation, direction, communication, relationships, and the movement of the Holy Spirit.

In another discourse, Jesus was relating physical and earthly things to heavenly things. He noted how cloud formations tell us that rain is coming and wind direction can tell us what type of weather to expect. Then he asked this question concerning revelation: **"You can discern the face of the sky and of the earth, but how is it you do not discern this time? Yes, and why, even of yourselves, do you not judge what is right?"** (Luke 12:56–57). He asked two questions here relating to the discernment of the Spirit and to seeing things from a heavenly perspective. Jesus was saying that there are signs meant for us to see in the spirit realm. We look today and see great movements in megachurches and tremendous crowds gathering at these churches and many ministries, but do we see any kind of revival occurring in our cities? Do we see people coming together and loving one another in the Church, black, white, and all cultures mixing and proclaiming Christ throughout a particular geographic area? Are these manifestations isolated to one church or one charismatic leader?

It would seem that with all the Christian books being published and with the abundance of large conferences taking place that promote the causes of the Kingdom, that our country would be really moving toward the Lord. But Jesus is asking if we are really seeing his signs. Can we see through the diversions of this world? Are we divided? Are we in a marketing, promotional methodology that is not of the Kingdom in its essence or in its manifestation? Are we, as Christ's designated messengers, creating change beneficial to his Kingdom, or has stagnancy taken hold, and is trouble brewing?

Jesus revealed himself following his resurrection to two men walking along a road. They were discussing the very popular and contentious subject of Jesus's crucifixion in spite of all his miraculous and life-giving works. Jesus, approaching from behind, asked them, **"What kind of conversation is this that you have with one another as you walk and are sad?"** (Luke 24:17). He went on to induce them into narrating their version of his recent plight in Jerusalem and how his body had disappeared from his tomb three days following his death. Jesus then asked them, **"Ought not the Christ to have suffered these things and to enter into his glory?"** (Luke 24:26).

Jesus chided them through his questions, wanting them to see how the Scriptures revealed his purpose. Then Jesus had a conversation with them, in which he explained everything Moses, the prophets, and everyone else had said about him throughout the Scriptures. As they began to approach the village, he was asked if he would stay with them for a little while, and he obliged. As they began to break bread, a sense of recognition washed over the two men, and Jesus abruptly disappeared. As they began to recount their time with him and the feeling they had while he was there, they had sensed his presence in a special way.

Although Christ is not physically present with us today, he is present spiritually. He dwells within us personally (John 15:1–4). He is present in the proclamation of his word (Matt 28:18–20). And he guides us into all truth that he has taught (John 14:26; 16:13). Of course, we have the subjective assurance in accordance with his objective word (John 15:7). According to the Barna research group, more than 50 percent of Americans say they are Christians. They may attend church occasionally or even regularly, but only 7 percent are evangelicals who believe in the infallible word of God and believe that they are mandated to share their faith as a requirement of their belief in Christ. This is a relatively insignificant number of believers, and thus Jesus may be asking us if we can really sense when he is with us and if we really recognize what he is all about.

Immediately after Jesus encountered the two men on the road, he appeared to his disciples. When they saw him, they were frightened, and they thought that they were seeing a ghost. He was supposed to have been crucified! He asked them: **"Why are you troubled? And why do doubts arise in your hearts?"** (Luke 24:38). He then urged them to touch him. This was Jesus, in his physical and earthly form, revealing himself to the disciples. Jesus knew that the disciples struggled with their faith just as many do today. So he implored them to put their hands on him, to feel his physical body. While this is not possible today, nonetheless, he is with us spiritually. He is, and always has been, here for us (Heb 13:5). Why do we still doubt him? He is the King of kings and Lord of lords, and he wants to reveal himself to us. If we only open our hearts and minds and have faith in him, he will speak to us (James 1:5–6).

Jesus revealed himself in a surprising development in Mark 9, starting with verse 33. His group was on its way to Capernaum, and when they arrived, he asked the disciples a question: **"What was it you disputed among yourselves on the road?"** (Mark 9:33). Jesus was not with them during their debate, and the disciples were embarrassed because Jesus was revealing the fact that he can hear and see all. The disciples didn't respond to his question because they happened to be arguing over which one of them was the greatest. Isn't that something we also do today? We seem to be arguing over trivialities such as who is the greatest among us, or who has the biggest and best church or the most ministries. We also have great Christian leaders who we pay money to hear, as well as megachurches that draw thousands of attendees. Yet

Jesus is still curious as to what we are talking about. Would we be embarrassed by this question, just as his disciples were, because we know our answer would not be pleasing to him?

After asking his unanswered question to the embarrassed disciples, Jesus explained to them that whoever desires to be first must actually be willing to put himself last and must be a servant to all. With this in mind, when we get to heaven, we might find people we might not have expected or noticed. We might expect to see prominent televangelists and charismatic leaders in the Church occupying a high place in heaven. But we might instead find someone we never even knew about, maybe a simple person who had a deep relationship with Jesus and who ministered to many. Jesus won't even ask us how big of a crowd we drew. Instead, he will ask us how many disciples we made or how many servants we raised up for him.

In another instance, after Jesus hinted at his impending death and resurrection, Jesus knew that the disciples wanted to ask him a question. He said, **"Are you inquiring among yourselves about what I said, 'A little while, and you will not see me; and again a little while, and you will see me'?"** (John 16:19). Jesus knew there was something they did not quite understand, just as we may have difficulty understanding today. Jesus thus explained that there would be weeping and mourning amongst his believers after his crucifixion, but their grief was to be short-lived. He then described how they would rejoice over his resurrection, and how their joy would not be taken away. Jesus promised them that they would be given whatever they asked for in his name and that their joy would be complete.

Jesus next began to express that a time would come when he would reveal himself even more clearly and that he would always be available to us through his Spirit. He wanted us to understand that he was providing for us the ability to come directly to the Father in prayer and have our needs met just by appealing to him and to his name! He will answer our prayers if we go to the Father in Jesus's name. When the Holy Spirit comes, we will be able to communicate with him, and we will have something that the world does not. God cares for us so much that we can go directly to him and receive everything that we need by just appealing to him in the name of Jesus.

Similarly, when Mary Magdalene was in the garden crying, she saw two angels seated where Jesus's body had been. When they asked why she was crying, she replied that the body of her Lord had been taken somewhere unbeknownst to her. Suddenly, she turned around and there was Jesus, and he asked the same question: **"Woman, why are you weeping? Whom are you seeking?"** (John 20:15). She still did not know who he was. She thought it was the gardener until Jesus said her name, causing her to recognize him. Likewise, Jesus is asking us what it is we are looking for, what it is that we need. He is always here with us. He is always available to us if we only turn to him.

Even if we have completely turned away from Jesus, even if we have become angry and begun to persecute the Church, we are able to repent and start fresh and anew. Paul (who was known as Saul at the time) persecuted Christians and put them in jail, and it seems he even had some of them killed. On the road to Damascus, Jesus appeared before Paul and asked him, **"Saul, Saul, why are you persecuting me?"** (Acts 9:4). This question was so powerful that Paul fell right to the ground. He just fell over, empowered by God. Maybe Jesus wants us to fall over. Maybe he is posing the exact same question to us today. Jesus revealed himself to Paul and then sent him out to do his will. He turned a hater and persecutor of Christ into his lifelong soldier, and Paul became the most prolific writer of the New Testament! This type of transformation is available to us today. Jesus urges us to make him Lord of our lives, and in return, we receive his protection and presence. It is the greatest *spiritual revelation* of all time!

8

Spiritual Warnings

A Glance into the Future

THE DEFINITION

Warn: To tell (a person) of a danger, coming evil, misfortune, etc; put on guard; caution; to caution about certain acts; admonish; to notify in advance; inform; to give (a person) notice to stay or keep (off, away, etc.).

WEBSTER'S NEW WORLD DICTIONARY

WARNINGS ARE a caution for the future. Jesus issued many warnings and spoke often about the problems that are in store for humanity. He spoke about the end times and also about the tribulation, which refers to the destruction that will ultimately descend upon mankind. During this time of tribulation, nation will rise against nation, there will be earthquakes and famine, love will wax cold, and hate will become predominant. Jesus even said that he felt sorry for those who were bearing children because of this time to come. He was very emphatic about warning us of the days to come. Although we may have yet to reach the terrible era that Jesus predicted, he still warns us about our present attitudes and how our future might be affected.

THE BRIDGE

Jesus cautions us about how to function in order to protect ourselves and to live a more prosperous life. The purpose for putting questions in this category is that Jesus definitely saw a cause-and-effect relationship between our actions and their repercussions. He showed how some of our methods of doing things may cause us problems and thus gives us indications of how to prevent those problems in our everyday life. He really is asking us to ponder these questions and to investigate them so that they penetrate our spirit, and we act accordingly in relationship to his warnings.

THE QUESTIONS

Many of the questions asked by Jesus were designed to present a message of warning. For instance, he once asked a large crowd of followers, **"Or what king, going to make war against another king, does not sit down first and consider whether he is able with ten thousand to meet him who comes against him with twenty thousand?"** (Luke 14:31). Jesus was pointing out the necessity of preparation and emphasizing the importance of knowing what to expect from a situation. In the case of the undermanned king, a thoroughly prepared plan was essential in order to best negotiate his dilemma. Jesus used this example to compel his followers to consider what he expects from us when we commit to being a part of his Kingdom.

Assuming we have committed ourselves to the Kingdom and are living the life we expected, wouldn't it make sense for Jesus to request our absolute dedication to him? Are we willing to give up everything for him? Jesus told his followers later in the same passage: "*So likewise, whoever of you does not forsake all that he has cannot be My disciple*" (Luke 14:33). He was urging his followers to really ponder the implications of totally committing oneself to him. We have not chosen the easy road by dedicating our lives to his cause. In every facet of life, understanding the implications of our decisions is critical to the process. Are we willing to acknowledge the consequences of our decisions? Is Jesus not asking us this very question right now?

This concept applies not only to those who have chosen to be part of his spiritual Kingdom as Jesus described it but also in regard to making decisions. We must consider our primary objective and decide if we are willing to make whatever sacrifice is necessary to achieve that objective. Are we willing to prioritize what we need to do? If we determine the cost as being too great and we don't feel we can make it, how can we most efficiently function in the life that we've chosen? These are pertinent questions, and there are costs involved in whatever we decide. If we don't understand the implications of the decisions we've made, we probably need to ask ourselves some other questions. What are the criteria, and what are the consequences of our decisions?

There is a story that Jesus told about a landowner who planted a vineyard and leased it to some vinedressers while he was away. He kept sending servants to see how things were going, and the vinedressers, who were functioning on his land, repeatedly killed his servants. So the landowner eventually sent his son, and they killed him also. Then Jesus asked: **"Therefore, when the owner of the vineyard comes, what will he do to those vinedressers?"** (Matt 21:40; Mark 12:9; Luke 20:15). Jesus was really referring to himself being sent by God the Father to the Jews and being rejected. He was giving them a warning. It is well known that the Jewish nation has gone through tremendous persecution. In fact, some forty years after the resurrection, the Roman Empire came and destroyed the whole city of Jerusalem, including the temple. Maybe Jewish persecution was a consequence of their collective decision to reject and crucify Jesus. Warnings always have implications of consequence.

The landowner in this parable represents the Lord Almighty, and he sent many prophets to warn the nation of Israel about the type of life that they should live and the type of commitment that should be made to him. Israel did not heed these warnings, and his own people ultimately crucified Jesus. Thus we must ask ourselves, what constitutes a proper recompense for murdering the Son of God? Jesus told us that if we believe in and accept him and acknowledge the sacrifice he made for us, we will have eternal life. He has implored us to make him Lord of our lives and to turn our lives over to him. When we have done so, he accepts our repentance, and we become part of his Kingdom. But there will always be vinedressers. Many are hungry for power, rebellious toward authority, and reject the very protection of the Kingdom that God has given us. Thus Jesus is asking what will become of those who do not accept the atonement of the cross? What do they deserve? He wants us to ask ourselves and others this question.

Jesus gave another warning, an admonishment to us when he said, "*Watch therefore, for you do not know what hour your Lord is coming. But know this, that if the master of the house had known what hour the thief would come, he would have watched and not allowed his house to be broken into*" (Matt 24:42–43). Jesus continued, asking, "**Who then is a faithful and wise servant, whom his master made ruler over his household, to give them food in due season?**" (Matt 24:45). Jesus then answered his own question by stating that the dutiful slave would be greatly blessed. Who is a faithful and wise servant, and what does it mean to be one? If we are servants in the Kingdom, what is he defining as faithful and wise? Jesus said that a faithful and wise servant is one whom his master makes ruler over his household. This is a direct implication that the Lord has given us authority. He has given us dominion over the affairs of this life and over the area with which he has charged us.

Jesus has given us a certain responsibility. Thus, in the text of the above question, he is saying that the wise and faithful are those whom he has put in charge, those who commit to the Kingdom. Jesus said that the diligent and faithful servant would be greatly blessed for doing what he is supposed to. This really is a metaphor, with Jesus representing the master and us as Christians representing the slave. He truly is blessed when we produce for his

Kingdom in the areas to which we have been assigned. However, Jesus also issued a warning about the slave who takes advantage of his master's absence by mistreating those whom he has authority over, or by associating with undesirables, or by living a self-centered lifestyle. This slave, representing those who have turned their back on God, will be punished accordingly

There seems to be a definite warning from Jesus that Kingdom life and the assignments we are given are very critical to him. We need to stay on the path and remain focused, as we can never know what moment in our lives we may die, and we do not want to be in the wrong place at the wrong time, doing the wrong thing.

In one very familiar Scripture, Jesus asked: **"For which of you, intending to build a tower, does not sit down first and count the cost, whether he has enough to finish it?"** (Luke 14:28). This question relates directly to the idea of sacrifice. When we commit our lives to Christ and dedicate ourselves to doing the work of his Kingdom, it is a life-changing event. In order to be utilized to our maximum potential within Christ's Kingdom, we must allow ourselves to become pliable and to put aside those things that were of importance to our former selves. This idea of sacrifice is inherent in the spiritual life. It is something we should evaluate thoroughly in relation to our own lives in order to determine if we are really willing to dedicate our total being to the causes of the Kingdom. It is to our detriment to make a half-hearted, ambivalent sort of commitment to Christ without considering what is really going to be expected of us.

Jesus was once told of an instance where Pilate had mixed the blood of some Galileans who had been killed with the blood of some animals being sacrificed. Jesus asked a question to those who told him this: **"Do you suppose that these Galileans were worse sinners than all other Galileans, because they suffered such things?"** (Luke 13:2). Jesus was questioning the ancient assumption that calamity would only befall those who were extremely sinful. If we go through suffering, whether we are believers or not, is it because we are worse than those who are not suffering? Jesus gave them an answer to his own question, an answer that should really give us pause. He pointed out that we are all sinners who must repent or face a fearful end. Jesus repeated this theme with a question similar to the one above: **"Or those eighteen on whom the tower in Siloam fell and killed them, do you think that they were worse sinners than all other men who dwelt in Jerusalem?"** (Luke 13:4). The point that he was making was that our life in the Kingdom has to be one of repentance and brokenness, not one of comparison to one another. Are we comparing ourselves to others for the sake of determining who is better or worse in the eyes of God? Jesus knows that we are all equally fallible and sinful as humans and thus need to repent equally, as we are all equal at the cross.

In one of the most expressive warnings implied by Jesus, He asked a question to the leaders of the religious system: **"Serpents, brood of vipers! How can you escape the condemnation of hell?"** (Matt 23:33). Before he asked this question, Jesus reminded these leaders of how they built and decorated the tombs of the prophets who had been persecuted and killed, and how these same leaders tried in vain to absolve themselves from incrimination by claiming that they would have never committed these acts toward the prophets had they been alive during that time. Jesus was quick to burst their bubble of self-righteousness by pointing out that they were every bit as complicit in carrying out the same type of persecution of God's people as their forefathers. This was a definitive warning to them that they would have been well served to heed.

We can ask this question to those involved in his work today. Have we become so self-righteous that our priorities are focused on the beauty, or attendance, or number of ministries we have in our churches? Are we also claiming that we're not going to do what the unrighteous have done? Perhaps we need to ask ourselves if we are doing what we are supposed to be doing. Maybe we are donating to foreign missions, but what are we doing in our own communities? Is the Church really uniting in our cities, with God's people laying down their lives for one another as in Acts 2:42, where Jesus's believers sold all their possessions and met daily in the temple? These believers completely came together, and their love for one another was a testimony to their discipleship under Jesus. Many people came into relationship with Jesus each day because they saw this tremendous testimony in Jerusalem. These believers were laying down their lives for each other, and when they encountered hardships, they all stuck together. Denominations didn't exist, and there were no divisions. Is this true in our cities today?

We see pastors everywhere who go off in different directions. Many don't even associate with one another. They don't even know each other. We rarely see pastors in each town going to each other's churches and preaching from different pulpits on Sunday mornings and sharing their perspective of the cause of Christ. We are divided as Christians, and thus Jesus would like to know how we expect to escape some form of rebuke if we act no differently than the world does. In fact, there may be other religions that do not even believe that Jesus is Lord and yet are much more unified and congruent than we are.

The disciples approached Jesus one day as he was leaving the temple and called his attention to its buildings. Jesus replied, **"Do you not see all these things?"** (Matt 24:2). He was referring to the enormity of the temple, which was comprised of a mammoth group of structures. Thousands could gather around it, and it would dwarf any church today by far, so it would be impossible to miss. Jesus then gave an explanation for his question, stating: *"Assuredly, I say to you, not one stone shall be left here upon another, that shall not be thrown down"* (Matt 24:2).

Jesus was not impressed with the activity in the temple, because many people worshipping inside of it were not sincere in their hearts or in their relationships, and they didn't even recognize him as Lord! So he issued this warning, stating that the building was self-serving and thus would eventually be destroyed. The Church is not about ornate buildings, it is not about programs, and it is not about functions. It is about relationships with God and his people. And relationships are being torn apart in the Church just as they are outside the Church. During the first few years of the twenty-first century, an average of 3,700 churches have closed their doors each year. If we focus on the building and we focus on programs and crowds, we completely miss the message Jesus came to deliver.

Jesus sometimes asked a question of a person in a parable for the sake of bringing the question to the forefront of his listener's conscience. As we have seen in other chapters, he often asked a question that others might ask him. He wanted us to enter the interrogative, to question ourselves along with our motives and our priorities. He wanted us to always seek out the spiritual meaning of things. In this text, he gave us a question that would be asked of him. He said, **"Many will say to me in that day, 'Lord, Lord, have we not prophesied in your name, cast out demons in your name, and done many wonders in your name?'"** (Matt 7:22). Weren't we involved with a church, dedicating ourselves to its programs and ministries?

Even so, this is not what Jesus valued most. He asks us to think about where we are today, to question our motives. Are we building buildings, or are we building relationships? Are we building ministries, or are we building families? Are we building programs, or are we building agreements, covenants, and sacrificing ourselves for our brothers and sisters? This is to be done not only in our own fellowship, so that our church looks better and more talented than the next, but with other churches and other members of the body of Christ outside of our own familiar and comfortable atmosphere. Are we letting our city know, our government know, the unbelievers know, the man on the street know, and those who belong to other religions know, that this Christian Church is *not* divided, but is in fact united?

Are we dealing with the issues that divide us? Is there sin in our camp? Are we addressing it? Are we coming together and deciding not to accept it? Do we act like one unified Church? Are we willing to lay down our lives for the pastor of the black AME or Missionary Baptist church and the Assembly of God church and the Southern Baptist church and the independent church? Can we discuss our differences? Are pastors from different churches offering their pulpits to one another? Only by fellowshipping with others outside of our comfort zone, and by holding others in higher esteem than ourselves, do we truly bless the Lord and act upon spiritual principles. Remember Jesus's words: "*Every kingdom divided against itself will be ruined, and every city or household divided against itself will not stand*" (Matt 12:25; NIV).

Jesus once said that we would be known by our fruit. If he walked into any city today, would he see the fruit of the Spirit in the corporate Church coming together and laying down its life for his cause? Would he see a glorious Church that he's looking to have a banquet with activating itself on this earth, or are we looking for crowds? Are we promoting ourselves as marketing instruments so that people will come to our church instead of another one? Do we feel that we've got an answer that someone else doesn't have? Or do we realize that many of our churches are just different personalities with different emphases? Yes, there are some errors, and it may take pain and conflict to work it out. That is what the Jerusalem Council was all about two thousand years ago (Acts 15). Bible-believing churches should not see themselves as more viable than the one down the street. We can learn from each other. We really do need to get together! Jesus does not want to scare us. These questions are to enlighten and provoke us together in love. It is a glance into the glorious Kingdom future as well as a *spiritual warning* to all churches in every city. Jesus cautions us today as he did the seven churches in the book of Revelation two thousand years ago.

Conclusion

WELL, NOW we have spent some time in the laboratory of questions. It is a realm Jesus created to help us contemplate his message deep in our spirits. Many of those who have desired to enter and expand their personal growth in this dimension called the Kingdom of God have developed a process called journaling.

Journaling is recording what we believe the Holy Spirit is speaking to us through his word. This accomplishes three things: First, it manifests that the Lord of the universe actually desires to speak to his people through his word, applying its truth to our lives. Second, when we write it down it reminds us of "what saith the Lord" to us. Finally, through this kind of devotional process, Jesus can answer all of the questions—at least those pertinent to our relationship to him. That is, I believe, how this book was written.

It is hard to imagine that Jesus just haphazardly asked all these questions without some purpose in mind. If we can draw any *spiritual conclusions* from this study, it may be Jesus is telling us, yes, he is the answer, but only if we learn from him to ask the question!

Appendix

QUESTIONS

In Chronological Order

Key

SA-Spiritual Alignment
SC-Spiritual Commitment
SL-Spiritual Life
SP-Spiritual Provisions
SR-Spiritual Relationships
SREV-Spiritual Revelations
SV-Spiritual Values
SW-Spiritual Warnings

1. "You are the salt of the earth; but if the salt loses its flavor, how shall it be seasoned?"

    Matthew 5:13; Mark 9:50; Luke 14:34 [SC]

2. "For if you love those who love you, what reward have you?"

    Matthew 5:46; Luke 6:32 [SR]

3. "Do not even the tax collectors do the same?"

    Matthew 5:46; Luke 6:32 [SR]

4. "And if you greet your brethren only, what do you do more than others?"

    Matthew 5:47 [SR]

5. "Do not even the tax collectors do so?"

    Matthew 5:47 [SR]

6. "Is not life more than food and the body more than clothing?"

> Matthew 6:25 [SV]

7. "Are you not of more value than they?"

> Matthew 6:26; Luke 12:24 [SV]

8. "Which of you by worrying can add one cubit to his stature?"

> Matthew 6:27; Luke 12:25 [SL]

9. "So why do you worry about clothing?"

> Matthew 6:28 [SL]

10. "Now if God so clothes the grass of the field, which today is, and tomorrow is thrown into the oven, will He not much more clothe you, O you of little faith?"

> Matthew 6:30; Luke 12:28 [SP]

11. "And why do you look at the speck in your brother's eye, but do not consider the plank in your own eye?"

> Matthew 7:3; Luke 6:41 [SR]

12. "Or how can you say to your brother, 'Let me remove the speck out of your eye'; and look, a plank is in your own eye?"

> Matthew 7:4; Luke 6:42 [SR]

13. "Or what man is there among you who, if his son asks for bread, will give him a stone?"

> Matthew 7:9; Luke 11:11 [SR]

14. "Or if he asks for a fish, will give him a serpent?"

> Matthew 7:10; Luke 11:11 [SR]

15. "Or if he asks for an egg, will he give him a scorpion?"

> Luke 11:12 [SR]

16. "Do men gather grapes from thorn bushes or figs from thistles?"

    Matthew 7:16 [SR]

17. "Many will say to Me in that day, 'Lord, Lord, have we not prophesied in Your name, cast out demons in Your name, and done many wonders in Your name?'"

    Matthew 7:22 [SW]

18. "Why are you fearful, O you of little faith?"

    Matthew 8:26; Mark 4:40; Luke 8:25 [SP]

19. "Why do you think evil in your hearts?"

    Matthew 9:4–5; Mark 2:8; Luke 5:22–23 [SP]

20. "For which is easier, to say, 'Your sins are forgiven you', or to say, 'Arise and walk'?"

    Matthew 9:4–5; Mark 2:8; Luke 5:22–23 [SP]

21. "Can the friends of the bridegroom mourn as long as the bridegroom is with them?"

    Matthew 9:15; Mark 2:19; Luke 5:43 [SR]

22. "Do you believe that I am able to do this?"

    Matthew 9:28 [SP]

23. "Are not two sparrows sold for a copper coin?"

    Matthew 10:29; Luke 12:6 [SP]

24. "What did you go out into the wilderness to see?"

    Matthew 11:7; Luke 7:24 [SR]

25. "A reed shaken by the wind?"

    Matthew 11:7; Luke 7:24 [SR]

26. "But what did you go out to see?"

    Matthew 11:8; Luke 7:25 [SR]

27. "A man clothed in soft garments?"

    Matthew 11:8; Luke 7:25 [SR]

28. "A prophet?"

> Matthew 11:9; Luke 7:26 [SR]

29. "But to what shall I liken this generation?"

> Matthew 11:16; Luke 7:31 [SR]

30. "Have you not read what David did when he was hungry, he and those who were with him: how he entered the house of God and ate the showbread which was not lawful for him to eat, nor for those who were with him, but only for the priests?"

> Matthew 12:3–4; Mark 2:25–26;
> Luke 6:3–4 [SR]

31. "Or have you not read in the law that on the Sabbath the priests in the temple profane the Sabbath, and are blameless?"

> Matthew 12:5 [SR/SL]

32. "What man is there among you who has one sheep, and if it falls into a pit on the Sabbath, will not lay hold of it and lift it out?"

> Matthew 12:11; Luke 14:5 [SV]

33. "Of how much more value then is a man than a sheep?"

> Matthew 12:12 [SV]

34. "Does not each one of you on the Sabbath loose his ox or his donkey from the stall and lead it away to water it?"

> Luke 13:15–16 [SV]

35. "So ought not this woman, being a daughter of Abraham, whom Satan has bound—think of it—for eighteen years, be loosed from this bond on the Sabbath?"

> Luke 13:15–16 [SV]

36. "How then will his kingdom stand?"

> Matthew 12:26 [SL]

Appendix 91

37. "If Satan also is divided against himself, how will his kingdom stand?"

    Luke 11:18 [SL]

38. "And if I cast out demons by Beelzebub, by whom do your sons cast them out?"

    Matthew 12:27; Luke 11:19 [SL]

39. "Or else how can one enter a strong man's house and plunder his goods, unless he first binds the strong man?"

    Matthew 12:29 [SL]

40. "How can you, being evil, speak good things?"

    Matthew 12:34 [SL]

41. "Who is My mother and who are My brothers?"

    Matthew 12:48; Mark 3:33 [SR]

42. "So the servants of the owner came and said to him, 'Sir, did you not sow good seed in your field'?"

    Matthew 13:27 [SP]

43. "How then does it have tares?"

    Matthew 13:27 [SP]

44. "The servants said to him, 'Do you want us then to go and gather them up'?"

    Matthew 13:28 [SL]

45. "Have you understood all these things?"

    Matthew 13:51 [SL]

46. "O you of little faith, why did you doubt?"

    Matthew 14:31 [SP]

47. "Why do you also transgress the commandment of God because of your tradition?"

    Matthew 15:3 [SR]

48. "Are you also still without understanding?"
> Matthew 15:16–17; Mark 7:18–19 [SL]

49. "Do you not yet understand that whatever enters the mouth goes into the stomach and is eliminated?"
> Matthew 15:16–17; Mark 7:18–19 [SL]

50. "How many loaves do you have?"
> Matthew 15:34; Mark 8:5 [SP]

51. "O you of little faith, why do you reason among yourselves because you have brought no bread?"
> Matthew 16:8; Mark 8:17 [SL]

52. "Why do you reason because you have no bread?"
> Matthew 16:8; Mark 8:17 [SREV]

53. "Do you not yet perceive nor understand?"
> Matthew 16:8; Mark 8:17 [SREV]

54. "Do you not yet understand, or remember the five loaves or the five thousand and how many baskets you took up?"
> Matthew 16:9; Mark 8:17 [SP]

55. "Is your heart still hardened?"
> Mark 8:17 [SREV]

56. "Having eyes, do you not see?"
> Mark 8:18 [SL/SP]

57. "And having ears, do you not hear?"
> Mark 8:18 [SL/SP]

58. "And do you not remember?"
> Mark 8:18 [SL/SP]

59. "When I broke the five loaves for the five thousand, how many baskets full of fragments did you take up?"
> Mark 8:19 [SL/SP]

Appendix 93

60. "Nor the seven loaves of the four thousand and how many large baskets you took up?"
>Matthew 16:10; Mark 8:20 [SP]

61. "How is it you do not understand that I did not speak to you concerning bread?"
>Matthew 11:11; Mark 8:21 [SW]

62. "Who do men say that I, the Son of Man, am?"
>Matthew 16:13; Mark 8:27; Luke 9:18 [SR]

63. "But who do you say that I am?"
>Matthew 16:15; Mark 8:29; Luke 9:20 [SR]

64. "For what is a man profited if he gains the whole world, and loses his own soul?"
>Matthew 16:26; Mark 8:36–37; Luke 9:25 [SV]

65. "Or what will a man give in exchange for his soul?"
>Matthew 16:26; Mark 8:36–37; Luke 9:25 [SV]

66. "O faithless and perverse generation, how long shall I be with you?"
>Matthew 17:17; Mark 9:19; Luke 9:41 [SP]

67. "How long shall I bear with you?"
>Matthew 17:17; Mark 9:19; Luke 9:41 [SP]

68. "What do you think, Simon?"
>Matthew 17:25 [SR]

69. "From whom do the kings of the earth take customs or taxes, from their own sons or from strangers?"
>Matthew 17:25 [SR]

70. "What do you think?"
>Matthew 18:12 [SR/SV]

71. "If a man has a hundred sheep, and one of them goes astray, does he not leave the ninety-nine and go to the mountains to seek the one that is straying?"

> Matthew 18:12 [SR/SV]

72. "Should you not also have had compassion on your fellow servant, just as I had pity on you?"

> Matthew 18:33 [SR]

73. "Have you not read that He who made them at the beginning 'made them male and female' and said, 'For this reason a man shall leave his father and mother and be joined to his wife, and the two shall become one flesh'?"

> Matthew 19:4–5 [SR]

74. "Why do you call Me good?"

> Matthew 19:17; Mark 10:18; Luke 18:19 [SV]

75. "And about the eleventh hour He went out and found others standing idle, and said to them, 'Why have you been standing here idle all day'?'"

> Matthew 20:6 [SP]

76. "Did you not agree with me for a denarius?"

> Matthew 20:13b [SP]

77. "Is it not lawful for Me to do what I wish with My own things?"

> Matthew 20:15 [SR]

78. "Or is your eye evil because I am good?"

> Matthew 20:15 [SR]

79. "What do you wish?"

> Matthew 20:21; Mark 10:36 [SR]

80. "Are you able to drink the cup that I am about to drink, and be baptized with the baptism that I am baptized with?"

> Matthew 20:22; Mark 10:38 [SC]

81. "What do you want Me to do for you?"

> Matthew 20:32; Mark 10:51; Luke 18:41 [SP]

82. "Have you never read, 'Out of the mouth of babes and nursing infants You have perfected praise'?"

> Matthew 21:16 [SR]

83. "The baptism of John, where was it from?"

> Matthew 21:25; Mark 11:29–30; Luke 20:3–4 [SA]

84. "From heaven or from men?"

> Matthew 21:25; Mark 11:29–30; Luke 20:3–4 [SA]

85. "But what do you think?"

> Matthew 21:28 [SC]

86. "Which of the two did the will of his father?"

> Matthew 21:31 [SC]

87. "Therefore, when the owner of the vineyard comes, what will he do to those vinedressers?"

> Matthew 21:40; Mark 12:9; Luke 20:15 [SW]

88. "Did you never read in the Scriptures: 'The stone which the builders rejected has become the chief cornerstone. This was the LORD'S doing, and it is marvelous in our eyes'?"

> Matthew 21:42; Mark 12:10–11; Luke 20:17 [SA]

89. "So he said to him, 'Friend, how did you come in here without a wedding garment'?"

> Matthew 22:12 [SA]

90. "Why do you test Me, you hypocrites?"

    Matthew 22:18; Mark 12:15; Luke 20:23 [SA]

91. "Whose image and inscription is this?"

    Matthew 22:20; Mark 12:16; Luke 20:24 [SA]

92. "But concerning the resurrection of the dead, have you not read what was spoken to you by God, saying, 'I am the God of Abraham, the God of Isaac, and the God of Jacob'?"

    Matthew 22:31–32; Mark 12:26 [SA]

93. "What do you think about the Christ?"

    Matthew 22:42 [SA]

94. "Whose Son is He?"

    Matthew 22:42 [SA]

95. "How then does David in the Spirit call Him 'Lord,' saying: 'The Lord said to my Lord, sit at My right hand, till I make Your enemies Your footstool'?"

    Matthew 22:43–44 [SA]

96. "If David then calls Him 'Lord,' how is He his Son?"

    Matthew 22:45; Mark 12:37; Luke 20:44 [SA]

97. "For which is greater, the gold or the temple that sanctifies the gold?"

    Matthew 23:17 [SV]

98. "For which is greater, the gift or the altar that sanctifies the gift?"

    Matthew 23:19 [SV]

99. "How can you escape the condemnation of hell?"

    Matthew 23:33 [SW]

100. "Do you not see all these things?"

    Matthew 24:2; Mark 13:2 [SW]

Appendix 97

101. "Who then is a faithful and wise servant, whom his master made ruler over his household, to give them food in due season?"

> Matthew 24:45; Luke 12:42 [SW]

102. "Then the righteous will answer Him, saying, 'Lord, when did we see You hungry and feed You, or thirsty and give You drink'?"

> Matthew 25:37 [SR]

103. "When did we see You a stranger and take You in, or naked and clothe You?"

> Matthew 25:38 [SR]

104. "Or when did we see You sick, or in prison, and come to You?"

> Matthew 25:39 [SR]

105. "Then they also will answer Him saying, 'Lord, when did we see You hungry or thirsty or a stranger or naked or sick or in prison, and did not minister to You'?"

> Matthew 25:44 [SR]

106. "Why do you trouble the woman?"

> Matthew 26:10; Mark 14:6 [SR/SA]

107. "What, could you not watch with Me one Hour?"

> Matthew 26:40 [SC]

108. "Simon, are you sleeping?"

> Mark 14:37 [SC]

109. "Could you not watch with Me one hour?"

> Mark 14:37 [SC]

110. "Are you still sleeping and resting?"

> Matthew 26:45; Mark 14:41; Luke 22:46 [SC]

111. "Friend, why have you come?"
> Matthew 26:50 [SR]

112. "Or do you think that I cannot now pray to My Father, and He will provide Me with more than twelve legions of angels?"
> Matthew 26:53 [SA]

113. "How then could the Scriptures be fulfilled, that it must happen thus?"
> Matthew 26:54 [SA]

114. "Have you come out, as against a robber, with swords and clubs to take Me?"
> Matthew 26:55; Mark 14:48 [SR]

115. "Eli, Eli, lama sabachthani?" that is *"My God, My God, why have You forsaken Me?"*
> Matthew 27:46; Mark 15:34 [SL]

116. "Is it lawful on the Sabbath to do good or to do evil, to save life or to kill?"
> Mark 3:4; Luke 6:9 Luke 14:3 [SR]

117. "How can Satan cast out Satan?"
> Matthew 12:26b; Mark 3:23 [SA]

118. "Do you not understand this parable?"
> Mark 4:13 [SL]

119. "How then will you understand all the parables?"
> Mark 4:13 [SL]

120. "Is a lamp brought to be put under a basket or under a bed?"
> Mark 4:21 [SC]

121. "Is it not to be set on a lampstand?"
> Mark 4:21 [SC]

Appendix 99

122. "To what shall we liken the kingdom of God?"
>Mark 4:30; Luke 13:18; Luke 13:20 [SL]

123. "Or with what parable shall we picture it?"
>Mark 4:30; Luke 13:18; Luke 13:20 [SL]

124. "What is you name?"
>Mark 5:9; Luke 8:30 [SR]

125. "Who touched My clothes?"
>Mark 5:30; Luke 8:45 [SR]

126. "Why make this commotion and weep?"
>Mark 5:39 [SL]

127. "How many loaves do you have?"
>Mark 6:38 [SL]

128. "Why does this generation seek a sign?"
>Mark 8:12 [SREV]

129. "Is our heart still hardened?"
>Mark 8:18 [SREV]

130. "Having eyes, do you not see?"
>Mark 8:18 [SREV]

131. "And having ears, do you not hear?"
>Mark 8:18 [SREV]

132. "And how is it written concerning the Son of Man, that He must suffer many things and be treated with contempt?"
>Mark 9:12 [SREV]

133. "What are you discussing with them?"
>Mark 9:16 [SL]

134. "How long has this been happening to him?"
>Mark 9:21 [SL]

135. "What was it you disputed among yourselves on the road?"

> Mark 9:33 [SREV]

136. "What did Moses command you?"

> Mark 10:3 [SV]

137. "Why do you call Me good?"

> Mark 10:18 [SV]

138. "Is it not written, 'My house shall be called a house of prayer for all nations'?"

> Mark 11:17 [SA]

139. "Are you not therefore mistaken, because you do not know the Scriptures nor the power of God?"

> Mark 12:24 [SA]

140. "How is it that the scribes say that the Christ is the Son of David?"

> Mark 12:35; Luke 20:41 [SA]

141. "Why is it that you sought Me?"

> Luke 2:49 [SR]

142. "Did you not know that I must be about My Father's business?"

> Luke 2:49 [SR]

143. "And if you do good to those who do good to you, what credit is that to you?"

> Luke 6:33 [SV]

144. "And if you lend to those from whom you hope to receive back, what credit is that to you?"

> Luke 6:34 [SV]

145. "Can the blind lead the blind?"

> Luke 6:39 [SL]

146. "Will they not both fall into the ditch?"

> Luke 6:39 [SL]

147. "But why do you call me 'Lord, Lord,' and not do the things which I say?"

> Luke 6:46 [SA]

148. "Tell Me, therefore, which of them will love him more?"

> Luke 7:42 [SR]

149. "Do you see this woman?"

> Luke 7:44 [SA]

150. "What is written in the law?"

> Luke 10:26 [SREV]

151. "What is your reading of it?"

> Luke 10:26 [SREV]

152. "So which of these three do you think was neighbor to him, who fell among the thieves?"

> Luke 10:36 [SR]

153. "Which of you shall have a friend, and go to him at midnight and say to him, 'Friend, lend me three loaves; for a friend of mine has come to me on his journey, and I have nothing to set before him'; and he will answer from within and say, 'Do not trouble me; the door is now shut, and my children are with me in bed; I cannot rise and give to you'?"

> Luke 11:5–7 [SR]

154. "Did not He who made the outside make the inside also?"

> Luke 11:40 [SW]

155. "Man, who made Me a judge or an arbitrator over you?"

> Luke 12:14 [SV]

156. "And he thought within himself, saying, 'What shall I do, since I have no room to store my crops'?"

>Luke 12:17 [SV]

157. "If you then are not able to do the least, why are you anxious for the rest?"

>Luke 12:26 [SL]

158. "Do you suppose that I came to give peace on earth?"

>Luke 12:51 [SC]

159. "You can discern the face of the sky and of the earth, but how is it you do not discern this time?"

>Luke 12:56 [SREV]

160. "Yes, and why, even of yourselves, do you not judge what is right?"

>Luke 12:57 [SREV]

161. "Do you suppose that these Galileans were worse sinners than all other Galileans, because they suffered such things?"

>Luke 13:2 [SW]

162. "Or those eighteen on whom the tower in Siloam fell and killed them, do you think that they were worse sinners than all other men who dwelt in Jerusalem?"

>Luke 13:4 [SW]

163. "Cut it down; why does it use up the ground?"

>Luke 13:17 [SW]

164. "For which of you, intending to build a tower, does not sit down first and count the cost, whether he has enough to finish it?"

>Luke 14:28 [SW]

Appendix 103

165. "Or what king, going to make war against another king, does not sit down first and consider whether he is able with ten thousand to meet him who comes against him with twenty thousand?"

    Luke 14:31 [SW]

166. "What man of you, having a hundred sheep, if he loses one of them, does not leave the ninety-nine in the wilderness, and go after the one which is lost until he finds it?"

    Luke 15:4 [SV]

167. "Or what woman, having ten silver coins, if she loses one coin, does not light a lamp, sweep the house, and seek diligently until she finds it?"

    Luke 15:8 [SV]

168. "Therefore if you have not been faithful in the unrighteous mammon, who will commit to your trust the true riches?"

    Luke 16:11–12 [SV]

169. "And if you have not been faithful in what is another man's, who will give you what is your own?"

    Luke 16:11–12 [SV]

170. "And which of you, having a servant plowing or tending sheep, will say to him when he has come in from the field, 'Come at once and sit down to eat'?"

    Luke 17:7 [SA]

171. "But will he not rather say to him, 'Prepare something for my supper, and gird yourself and serve me till I have eaten and drunk, and afterward you will eat and drink'?"

    Luke 17:8 [SA]

172. "Does he thank that servant because he did the things that were commanded him?"

    Luke 17:9 [SA]

173. "Were there not ten cleansed?"
>Luke 17:17 [SV]

174. "But where are the nine?"
>Luke 17:17 [SV]

175. "Were there not any found who returned to give glory to God except this foreigner?"
>Luke 17:18 [SV]

176. "And shall God not avenge His own elect who cry out day and night to Him, though He bears long with them?"
>Luke 18:7 [SR]

177. "Nevertheless, when the Son of Man comes, will He really find faith on the earth?"
>Luke 18:8 [SR]

178. "Why then did you not put my money in the bank, that at my coming I might have collected it with interest?"
>Luke 19:23 [SV]

179. "For who is greater, he who sits at the table, or he who serves?"
>Luke 22:27 [SV]

180. "Is it not he who sits at the table?"
>Luke 22:27 [SV]

181. "When I sent you without money bag, knapsack, and sandals, did you lack anything?"
>Luke 22:35 [SP]

182. "Judas, are you betraying the Son of Man with a kiss?"
>Luke 22:48 [SREV]

Appendix 105

183. "For if they do these things in the green wood, what will be done in the dry?"

> Luke 23:31 [SL]

184. "What kind of conversation is this that you have with one another as you walk and are sad?"

> Luke 24:17 [SREV]

185. "What things?"

> Luke 24:19 [SREV]

186. "Ought not the Christ to have suffered these things and to enter into His glory?"

> Luke 24:26 [SREV]

187. "Why are you troubled?"

> Luke 24:38 [SREV]

188. "And why do doubts arise in your hearts?"

> Luke 24:38 [SREV]

189. "Have you any food here?"

> Luke 24:41 [SL]

190. "What do you seek?"

> John 1:38 [SA]

191. "Woman, what does your concern have to do with Me?"

> John 2:4 [SA]

192. "Are you the teacher of Israel, and do not know these things?"

> John 3:10 [SREV]

193. "If I have told you earthly things and you do not believe, how will you believe if I tell you heavenly things?"

> John 3:12 [SREV]

194. "Do you not say, 'There are still four months and then comes the harvest'?"

> John 4:35 [SP]

195. "Do you want to be made well?"

> John 5:6 [SP]

196. "How can you believe, who receive honor from one another, and do not seek the honor that comes from the only God?"

> John 5:44 [SA]

197. "But if you do not believe his writings, how will you believe My words?"

> John 5:47 [SREV]

198. "Where shall we buy bread, that these may eat?"

> John 6:5 [SP]

199. "Does this offend you?"

> John 6:61 [SREV]

200. "What then if you should see the Son of Man ascend where He was before?"

> John 6:62 [SA]

201. "Do you also want to go away?"

> John 6:67 [SR]

202. "Did I not choose you, the twelve, and one of you is a devil?"

> John 6:70 [SREV]

203. "Did not Moses give you the law, and yet none of you keeps the law?"

> John 7:19 [SC]

204. "Why do you seek to kill me?"

> John 7:19 [SA]

205. "If a man receives circumcision on the Sabbath, so that the law of Moses should not be broken, are you angry with Me because I made a man completely well on the Sabbath?"

        John 7:23 [SP]

206. "Woman, where are those accusers of yours?"

        John 8:10 [SR]

207. "Has no one condemned you?"

        John 8:10 [SR]

208. "Why do you not understand My speech?"

        John 8:43 [SR]

209. "Which of you convicts Me of sin?"

        John 8:46 [SR]

210. "And if I tell the truth, why do you not believe Me?"

        John 8:46 [SR]

211. "Do you believe in the Son of God?"

        John 9:35 [SA]

212. "For which of those works do you stone Me?"

        John 10:32 [SA]

213. "Is it not written in your law, 'I said, You are gods'?"

        John 10:34 [SA]

214. "If He called them gods, to whom the word of God came (and the Scripture cannot be broken), do you say of Him whom the Father sanctified and sent into the world, 'You are blaspheming,' because I said, 'I am the Son of God'?"

        John 10:35–36 [SA]

215. "Are there not twelve hours in the day?"

        John 11:9 [SC]

216. "Do you believe this?"

> John 11:26 [SA]

217. "Where have you laid him?"

> John 11:34 [SR]

218. "Did I not say to you that if you would believe you would see the glory of God?"

> John 11:40 [SR]

219. "Now My soul is troubled, and what shall I say? 'Father, save Me from this hour'?"

> John 12:27 [SC]

220. "Do you know what I have done to you?"

> John 13:12 [SR]

221. "Will you lay down you life for My sake?"

> John 13:38 [SC]

222. "Have I been with you so long, and yet you have not known Me, Philip?"

> John 14:9 [SR]

223. "He who has seen Me has seen the Father; so how can you say, 'Show us the Father'?"

> John 14:9 [SREV]

224. "Do you not believe that I am in the Father, and the Father in Me?"

> John 14:10 [SREV]

225. "Are you inquiring among yourselves about what I said, 'A little while, and you will not see Me; and again a little while, and you will see Me'?"

> John 16:19 [SREV]

226. "Do you now believe?"

> John 16:31 [SC]

227. "Whom are you seeking?"

> John 18:4; John 18:7 [SA]

228. "Shall I not drink the cup which My Father has given Me?"

> John 18:11 [SA]

229. "Why do you ask Me?"

> John 18:21 [SA]

230. "If I have spoken evil, bear witness of the evil; but if well, why do you strike Me?"

> John 18:23 [SA]

231. "Are you speaking for yourself on this, or did others tell you this about Me?"

> John 18:34 [SREV]

232. "Woman, why are you weeping?"

> John 20:15 [SREV]

233. "Whom are you seeking?"

> John 20:15 [SREV]

234. "Children, have you any food?"

> John 21:5 [SREV]

235. "Simon son of Jonah, do you love Me more than these?"

> John 21:15 [SREV]

236. "Simon, son of Jonah, do you love Me?"

> John 21:16 [SREV]

237. "Simon, son of Jonah, do you love Me?"

> John 21:17 [SREV]

238. "If I will that he remain till I come, what is that to you?"

> John 21:22; John 21:23 [SA]

239. "Saul, Saul, why are you persecuting Me?"
>Acts 9:4; Acts: 22:7; Acts: 26:14 [SREV]

Note

Not all of the questions listed above are referenced in "The Question".

Scripture references may vary in wording in parallel passages of the Bible.

Scriptures may pertain to more than one Spiritual aspect of life, thereby referencing more than one Spiritual key code.

www.ingramcontent.com/pod-product-compliance
Lightning Source LLC
Chambersburg PA
CBHW070925160426
43193CB00011B/1584